HORACE MANN,

THE EDUCATOR.

By ALBERT E. WINSHIP.

BOSTON:
NEW ENGLAND PUBLISHING CO.
1896.

Horace Mann

To Henry Barnard,

THE

MOST DISTINGUISHED EDUCATIONAL CONTEMPORARY

OF

HORACE MANN,

AND THE

MOST EMINENT LIVING EDUCATOR, THIS TRIBUTE TO

MR. MANN IS AFFECTIONATELY

DEDICATED BY THE

AUTHOR.

PREFACE.

Great men are rare. Mute, inglorious Miltons may be numerous, but greatness, as the world views it, must be judged from the way in which emergencies are met. Horace Mann was a great educator because he met a great educational emergency.

With some characters greatness is linked to a single event. Columbus discovered America, Wellington defeated Napoleon at Waterloo, Perry wrote, " We met the enemy and they are ours." With others it is an inherited reputation of which few have any definite estimate as to the merit of the popular verdict. Walpole and Pitt in England, John Hancock and Charles Sumner in America are securely anchored in the public mind though few can give a reason for the admiration that is in them. Horace Mann's reputation is largely of the latter class. His name is a household word among teachers and yet few can tell aught of the man or of his work.

The one hundredth anniversary of his birth (May 4, 1896) should make this entire year a memorial season so far as to give every teacher and every school acquaintance with the essential features of his character and with the leading characteristics of his work.

There is one great monument to this leader in the " Life and Works of Horace Mann," in five volumes edited by his widow and published by Lee & Shepard, Boston. Without these volumes comparatively little could now be written of his life. His correspondence was voluminous and confidential, giving details regarding his contests and he was one of the few men fortunate enough to keep a good diary. The correspondence and the diary were both available when Mrs. Mann wrote this " Life," and for the service here rendered the educational public owes her a debt of gratitude. These volumes also contain his reports and addresses. Unfortunately many who would gladly know of Horace Mann cannot afford to buy the five volumes, and many will regret that they do not contain the great controversy with the " Thirty-one Boston Masters."   An inexpensive book upon " Horace Mann, the Educator " should certainly be available.

The author would acknowledge his indebtedness to the " Life and Works " by Mrs. Mann.   No apology is made for the absence of reference footnotes—since no claim is entered to skill in " the laboratory method in history," nor for the absence of a literary or historical style which requires the pruning and polishing of sentences; nor for the unusual freedom in the expression of opinion. The facts are closely verified, the winnowing has been done with some care, whatever bears no relation to his educational service being eliminated.   Beyond that the thought has been to give the author's view of the man, his work and his times in a condensed and readable form, with convictions rather than pretensions.

CONTENTS.

CHAPTER I.

By universal consent Horace Mann is the educator of the century. His is the name to conjure with in the forests of Michigan or the everglades of Florida, in the council of London or with the ministry of Prussia. People in school and out know that Washington is the father of his country, Lincoln the savior of the Union, Franklin the revealer of electricity, Webster the orator, and Horace Mann the educator. But, alas, they do not know much about this educator or his work. The most prominent statue in Boston, placed by the Commonwealth in front of the state house is an imposing bronze figure of Horace Mann. His twelve reports to the State Board of Education are the rarest and most valuable educational works in our language.

Hon. Anson P. Burlingame was a visitor at a session of the London city council when an educational appropriation was voted down by a decided majority. Then a member arose and read extracts from one of the reports of Horace Mann whereupon the city council of London reconsidered its action and made the appropriation. Such was the influence of Horace Mann in foreign parts.

After his retirement from office, business men of Boston presented him with a purse of two thousand dollars as a slight token of their appreciation of the service he had rendered the cause of education.

Why should one man, in no adequate sense a

teacher or a philosopher, no single sentence of
whose writings lives as the keynote to his service
or wisdom, be singled out to carry the honor and
exert the educational influence of the century
in American life? It is easier to ask this question
than to answer it. No one has yet analyzed that
strain in human nature by which Washington
carries in his name the honor and glory of the heroic generals, statesmen and patriots of the Revolution, or Grant the generalship of the Civil War
or John Brown the abolition enthusiasm of his
time. There are always many men who con-
tribute to the success of any great cause, and
some one among them receives the honor won by
all. In that great educational contest out of
which the normal schools were born and the
common school system of Massachusetts developed, Cyrus Pierce was the great teacher, Edmund Dwight the organizer of the State Board
of Education, and the founder of the normal
schools through his gift of $10,000, but the devo-
tion of Charles Sumner, Theodore Parker, and
Samuel J. May, the benefactions of Edmund
Dwight and Josiah Quincy, and the administra-
tive wisdom of Barnas Sears and George S. Bout-
well are all merged in the name of Horace Mann.
This could not be changed if we would. Who
would change it if he could?

There must be some reason for this trait in
human nature. There must have been something in the personality or experience of Mr. Mann
to give him such distinction. It is safe to say
that no teacher could have won such laurels, nor
could he have earned his permanent distinction
merely as secretary of the Board of Education.
While he did not owe his reputation to his elo-
quence, literary brilliancy, professional training,
statesmanship, religious conviction, temperance
zeal, abolition enthusiasm, or personal friend-

ships, he could not have been what he was with any of these factors omitted.

It is customary for the uninformed to attribute Mr. Mann's eminence to the fact that he sacrificed brilliant professional and political prospects to devote himself to the cause of education, and to consider this honor the due reward of such sacrifice. This is only partly true. He was a Boston lawyer and president of the Massachusetts Senate when he accepted the secretaryship of the Board of Education at a salary of $1,500 a year; but there was no prospect of immediate political advancement for him, and for the last three years of his practice he had slept in his little law office, and more than one-half the days found him without sufficient money to buy even a meagre luncheon. This last fact was due partly to his light income, but more to the heavy indebtedness incurred by indorsing for a brother, whose financial failure placed heavy burdens upon him. Again, he had every reason to suppose that the salary would be $2,500 the first year and rise to $3,000. There were greater sacrifices than he anticipated. The opportunity developed elements of character, brilliant talents of voice and pen, intensified the friendships of such men as Josiah Quincy, Charles Sumner, Henry Wilson, Edward Everett, and Theodore Parker, and ultimately won for him such personal and political popularity as to give him the seat in Congress when John Quincy Adams fell in his place in the National House of Representatives, and enabled him to secure reëlection against the most tyrannical dictation of Daniel Webster and the entire political management at his command.

If I may be allowed to put in a single phrase my estimate of the characteristics that made Mr. Mann an educational leader I would say it was his power to make and command a crisis.

CHAPTER II.

On March 2, 1778, an exceptionally intelligent village in Southern Massachusetts was incorporated as a town and was named after that great genius and statesman, Benjamin Franklin. Some enterprising citizen sent word to Mr. Franklin that it would give great satisfaction to the people if he would present to the town a bell for the church, in appreciation of the honor. Mr. Franklin said that he hoped a people who would name a town for him would have more regard for "sense than sound" and he preferred to give them a public library of five hundred volumes. Eighteen years later, May 4, 1796, Horace Mann was born in a humble farmhouse, and that library of Franklin's was the chief factor in giving the world the studious, scholarly, devoted, aggressive educational leader of America.

Until nearly twenty years of age he never went to school more than a few weeks in midwinter, and then to instructors who were "very good people but very poor teachers." The town did not then furnish "free text-books" and the lad worked many a half-day braiding straw for hats to get the money to buy spelling-book, arithmetic and reader. His father died when he was but thirteen and the boy worked thereafter for the support of the family.

When nearly twenty he came to know an inspiring classical teacher who convinced him that a college course was possible, and within six months from the time he first saw a Latin grammar he was admitted to the sophomore class of Brown University. It was such a six months of study as has rarely been known in America, and it broke his health for life. Nor was this the only evidence of the scholastic strength and brilliancy of Horace Mann. Although he entered the class with no adequate preparation and no literary culture, with all the traditional prejudices against the "short cut" students and those uncultured, he soon led his class and graduated far in advance of any other student. Upon graduating at the age of twenty-three, he remained at Brown as an instructor in Greek and Latin for three years. During his college years he taught country schools a few weeks each winter.

Through life, Horace Mann was inclined to refer to the trials and denials of his boyhood, to the poor teaching and lack of opportunities as great misfortunes, causing irreparable loss; but it is an open question whether he did not owe more to the first twenty years of his life in which there was developed hunger for knowledge, craving for opportunity which necessitated his reading histories and other works adapted to men rather than children, listening to such mighty sermons as only an Emmons of that day could preach,— thinking upon and rebelling against them all the week,—than he could have owed to any method of instruction that would have monopolized his thought or, rather, have diverted his mind to books or even to nature through these years.

From the day he entered college, he never had an hour for his mind to lie fallow. Speaking of these years he said,—"Yet with these obstructions, I had a love of knowledge which nothing could repress. An inward voice raised its plaint forever in my heart for something nobler and better; and if my parents had not the means to give me knowledge, they intensified the love of it.

They always spoke of learning and learned men
with enthusiasm and a kind of reverence. I was
taught to take care of the few books we had, as
though there was something sacred about them.
I never dog-eared one in my life, nor profanely
scribbled upon title-pages, margin, or fly-leaf; and
would as soon have stuck a pin through my flesh
as through the pages of a book."

All this denial and his life with his mother produced a character of which any man might well
be proud. "I have always been exempt from
what may be called common vices. I was never
intoxicated in my life; unless, perchance, with joy
or anger. I never swore; indeed, profanity was
always most disgusting and repulsive to me. And
(I consider it almost a climax) I never used the
'vile weed' in any form. I early formed the reso-
lution to be a slave to no habit." Speaking in
later life of his youthful longing for more education, he said,—"I know not how it was; its motive
never took the form of wealth or fame. It was
rather an instinct which impelled towards knowledge, as that of migratory birds impels them
northward in springtime. All my boyish castles
in the air had reference to doing something for
the benefit of mankind. The early precepts of
benevolence, inculcated upon me by my parents,
flowed out in this direction; and I had a conviction that knowledge was my needed instrument."

Referring to his financial limitations in college,
he wrote his sister at the time,—"If the children
of Israel were pressed for 'gear' half so hard as
I have been, I do not wonder they were willing to
worship a golden calf. It is a long time since my
last ninepence bade good-by to its brethren; and
I suspect the last two parted on no very friendly
terms, for they have never since met together.
Poor wretches! never did two souls stand in
greater need of mutual support and consolation."

No study of the life of Horace Mann would be complete that left out his tribute to his mother, for whom he worked and with whom he lived so incessantly after the death of his father. "Principle, duty, gratitude, affection, have bound me so closely to that parent whom alone Heaven has spared me, that she seems to me rather a portion of my own existence than a separate and independent being. I can conceive no emotions more pure, more holy, more like those which glow in the bosom of a perfected being, than those which a virtuous son must feel towards an affectionate mother. She has little means of rendering him assistance in his projects of aggrandizement, or in the walks of ambition; so that his feelings are uncontaminated with any of those earth-born passions that sometimes mingle their alloy with his other attachments. How different is the regard which springs from benefits which we hope hereafter to enjoy, from that which arises from services rendered and kindnesses bestowed even before we were capable of knowing their value! It is this higher sentiment that a mother challenges in a son. For myself, I can truly say that the strongest and most abiding incentive to excellence by which I was ever animated, sprang from that look of solicitude and hope, that heavenly expression of maternal tenderness, when, without the utterance of a single word, my mother has looked into my face, and silently told me that my life was freighted with a two-fold being, for it bore her destiny as well as my own. And as truly can I say that the most exquisite delight that ever thrilled me was, when some flattering rumor of myself had found its way to her ear, to mark her readier smile, her lighter step, her disproportionate encomiums on things of trivial value, when I was secretly conscious that her altered mien was caused by the fountains

of pleasure that were pouring their sweet waters
over her heart."

Mr. Mann's theme for his valedictory at gradua-
tion was "The Progressive Character of the Human Race." This was really the one theme upon
which he wrote and thought and talked through
life. At the age of twenty-five, he entered the law
school at Litchfield, Conn. One of his mates at
the law school has described him as a young man
with massive brow, high arching head, and mild
bright eye. He ranked as the best whist player
and the best lawyer in the institution. His training for his profession fitted him for a life of miscellaneous usefulness and occasional brilliancy
rather than for that of a plodding lawyer, for
devotion to humanity rather than to professional
aspiration.

Ten years of legislative life must demoralize
the professional practice of any thoroughly conscientious and honorable man. Legislative experience to be of professional advantage must
be associated with the business side of the legis-
lation rather than the philanthropic. Mr. Mann's
legislative tastes, convictions and associations
were better adapted to make him useful to humanity than financially successful as a lawyer.

CHAPTER III.

At the age of twenty-seven, Mr. Mann was admitted to the bar and began practice in Dedham. While never a great success financially, the court records show that he won four out of five of the cases that he tried. It was a financial misfortune that he would never try a case in which he did not believe that he was in the right. He fully appreciated that a man will pay a much larger sum to have a wrong cause advocated than a right, and that it lessens the popularity of an attorney to be thought good rather than smart, to care more for being right than for winning. In the fourteen years, he seems never to have had a case that brought him large returns or high honors, but his record for winning his cases has few parallels. He held that an advocate loses his highest power when he loses the ever-conscious conviction that he is contending for the truth; that though the fees or fame may be a stimulus, yet that a conviction of being right is itself creative of power, and renders its possessor more than a match for antagonists otherwise greatly his superiors. He used to say that in his conscious conviction of right there was a magnetism; and he only wanted an opportunity to be put in communication with a jury in order to impregnate them with his own belief. Beyond this, his aim always was, before leaving any head or topic in his argument, to condense its whole force into a vivid epigrammatic point, which the jury could not help remembering when they got into the jury-room; and, by graphic illustration and simile, to fasten pictures upon their minds, which they would retain and reproduce after abstruse arguments were forgotten. He endeavored to give to each one of the jurors something to be "quoted" on his side, when they retired for consultation. He argued his cases as though he was in the jury-room itself, taking part in the deliberations that were to be held there. From the confidence in his honesty, and those pictures with which he filled the air of the jury-room, came his uncommon success. The fourth year in Dedham he was elected to the Legislature, and his first speech was one of those masterly efforts which establish a reputation that endures.

Most of the misfortune that came to Mr. Mann in public life was associated directly or indirectly with his religious views. The mighty preaching of Doctor Emmons turned him, as a youth, against the evangelical faith, and inspired a purpose to champion liberality of thought on every occassion.

His first legislative honors were won, in 1827, in his great speech in defence of religious liberty in opposition to a scheme by which close corporations could secure the income of certain property forever to the support of particular creeds. From that hour he was again and again bitterly antagonized by the evangelical press and leaders, while at the same time he was unable to retain the unwavering support of those whom he championed.

His last days were saddened beyond description by a cruel sentence written by Theodore Parker, one of his best friends, in which he expressed regret at Mr. Mann's religious attitude at Antioch College, saying that he regretted that Mr. Mann had forgotten that in religion as in mathematics a straight line is the shortest distance between two points.

The town of Dedham did him the honor to send him to the Legislature for six successive years, as long indeed as he lived in that town. At the age of thirty-seven (1833) he moved to Boston, and the same year that senatorial district honored him, as few have been honored in political life, by sending him immediately to the State Senate, where he remained four years, the last two years as president of that body.

During his legislative life he gave much attention to philanthropic matters, especially to those connected with the care of the defective classes. To him was largely due the establishment of the Worcester Lunatic Asylum. He was one of the most ardent champions in the cause of the deaf and dumb. While engaged in efforts to ameliorate the condition of the unfortunate classes he became convinced that the greatest need in America was the better education of all children and youth; and he became the legislative champion of the plans of Edmund Dwight, James G. Carter and Robert Rantoul, Jr., for the establishment of a Board of Education.

During his college course he became much attached to the young daughter of Doctor Messer in whose family he lived, and ten years later, while he was practising law in Dedham, she became his wife. Speaking of her an intimate friend said, "When I knew his wife personally (I had long known her through him) I was indeed rejoiced that such an angelic being had been created to be his comfort, solace, joy and happiness. She was extremely delicate in health, and called forth the tenderest care. This fostering, protecting, caressing care, she had, of course, in perfection."

Their life together was brief, and when she died, it seemed as though there was for him no consolation. He describes his emotions as no

one else could do: "Amid the current of conversation, in social intercourse or the avocations of
business, in the daily walk of life, it is never but
half forgotten; and the sight of an object, the
utterance of a word, the tone of a voice, re-opens
upon me the mournful scene, and spreads around
me with electric quickness, a world of gloom.
During that period, when, for me, there was a
light upon earth brighter than any light of the
sun, and a voice sweeter than any of Nature's
harmonies, I did not think but that the happiness
which was boundless in present enjoyment would
be perpetual in duration. Do not blame my
ungrateful heart for not looking beyond the boon
with which Heaven had blessed me; for you know
not the potency of that enchantment. My life
went out of myself. One after another, the feelings which had before been fastened upon other
objects loosened their strong grasp, and went to
dwell in the sanctuary of her holy and beautiful
nature. Ambition forgot the applause of the
world for the more precious gratulations of that
approving voice. Joy ceased its quests abroad;
for at home there was an exhaustless fountain
to slake its renewing thirst. There imagination
built her palaces, and garnered her choicest treasures. She too supplied me with new strength for
toil and new motives for excellence. Within her
influence, there could be no contest for sordid
passions or degrading appetites; for she sent a
divine and overmastering strength into every
generous sentiment, which I cannot describe.
She purified my conceptions of purity, and beauti-
fied the ideal of every excellence. I never knew
her to express a selfish or an envious thought;
nor do I believe that the type of one was ever
admitted to disturb the peacefulness of her bosom.
Yet, in the passionate love she inspired, there was
nothing of oblivion of the rest of mankind. Her

teachings did not make one love others less, but differently, more aboundingly. Her sympathy with other's pain seemed to be quicker and stronger than the sensation of her own; and with a sensibility that would sigh at a crushed flower, there was a spirit of endurance that would uphold a martyr. There was in her breast no scorn of vice, but a wonder and amazement that it could exist. To her it seemed almost a mystery; and though she comprehended its deformity, it was more in pity than in indignation that she regarded it: but that hallowed joy with which she contemplated whatever tended to ameliorate the condition of mankind, to save them from pain or rescue them from guilt, was, in its manifestations, more like a vision from a brighter world, a divine illumination, than like the earthly sentiment of humanity." It was this affliction and the sadness with which it shrouded his life that led his friends to insist that he leave Dedham and take up life anew in Boston. There are few more heartrending scenes in life than the picture of this man leaving such a home and living in practical poverty, sleeping in his law office, the only person in the building, and, as he said, going without luncheon half the time because he could not afford the indulgence. There is very little satisfaction in the thought that one of the causes of this denial was the misfortune of a brother for whose debts he had become responsible. All these conditions made it easy for him to be tempted from law to semi-official life as secretary of the State Board of Education.

CHAPTER IV.

The cause of education might never have had Horace Mann as its great champion but for this combination of circumstances,—financial embarrassment, the absence of the cheer, the comforts and the necessities of home, and the bringing to a close of a legislative career of ten years. While he did not seek the secretaryship of the Board of Education, it was brought to his attention at a time when he must practically reënter upon the practice of law, which had for him very little attraction. He enjoyed individual cases but not the practice of law in the abstract. Writing on June 19, 1837, the very time that Edmund Dwight was urging upon him the consideration of the secretaryship, Mr. Mann said: "Employed the whole day in looking up a technical question of law. I have not, therefore, had anything in my head but technical combinations of technicalities. This part of the law has a strong tendency to make the mind nearsighted. What Coleridge says generally, and very untruly, of the law may be just when applied solely to this part of it,— that its operation upon the mind is like that of a grindstone upon a knife; it narrows while it sharpens. And is it not true that every object of science, however grand or elevated, has its atoms, its minute and subtle divisions and discriminations? The degrees of longitude upon the earth's surface, the zones into which the globe has been divided, and their corresponding lines and compartments in the heavens, would show pretty well in the registry for county deeds; but yet, in surveying and affixing the bounds and limits to these vast tracts of space, what minute calculations must the geographer and astronomer make! what fractions, what decimals, what infinitesimals! So the natural philosopher, whose patrimony, bequeathed to him by science, is continents and oceans and suns, must deal also with globules and animalculæ, and points vanishing into nothingness. Who can have more subtle questions to settle than the casuist or the metaphysician? So of all. In one direction we lose everything in magnificence, in vastness, in infinity; in the other direction we are equally lost in attempting to trace to their elements those substances, whatever they are, whose aggregate is earth, ocean, air, sky, immensity. Those who see nothing in the law but technicalities, *apices*, and *summa jura*, are about as wise as the child who mistook the infinite host of the stars for brass nails that fastened up the earth's ceiling." The next day he wrote: "Another day in search of the technical rules of law. If the whole professional business of a lawyer consisted only in investigating and determining technical rules, one might almost be excused for attempting to reach justice summarily through the instrumentality of that monster, a mob. Those who only have to pay for technical law are comparatively fortunate; but this effort for two days in succession to keep the eye fixed on the edge of a razor is apt to make one a little nervous."

Although he always tried to find satisfaction in the general advantages of law it was easy to see to what extent it bored him at the very time when Mr. Dwight was urging him to accept the secretaryship of the Board. It ought in fairness to be said that whenever he had a case it absorbed all his thought and energy for the time being. He had this to say at one time regarding the intensity of his devotion to every case that he had in hand: "The truth is that hearing common sermons gives my piety the consumption. Ministers seem to me not to care half so much about the salvation of mankind as I do about a justice's case. When I have a case before a justice of the peace I can't help thinking of it beforehand, and perhaps feeling grieved too, afterward, if in any respect I might have conducted it better. If I am at dinner, the merriment or the philosophy of the table-talk suggests something, which I put away into a pigeon-hole in my mind for the case; and when I read, be it poetry or prose, the case hangs over the page like a magnet, and attracts to itself whatever seems to be pertinent or applicable. Success or failure leaves a bright or a dark hue on my mind, often for days."

The attractions of his profession lessened as the temptation to the secretaryship increased. Mr. Mann inclined to accept the position on the ground of adaptability to his taste and desires before he could bring himself to admit that he was equal to its responsibilities. In his personal diary, intended for no eyes but his own, he wrote: "Ought I to think of filling this high and responsible office? Can I adequately perform its duties? Will my greater zeal in the cause than that of others supply the deficiency in point of talent and information? Whoever shall undertake that task must encounter privation, labor, and an infinite annoyance from an infinite number of schemers. He must condense the steam of enthusiasts, and soften the rock of the incredulous. What toil in arriving at a true system himself! what toil in infusing that system into the minds of others! How many dead minds to be resuscitated! how many prurient ones to be soothed! How much of mingled truth and error to be decompounded and analyzed! What a spirit of perseverance would be needed to sustain him all the way between the inception and the accomplishment of his objects! But should he succeed; should he bring forth the germs of greatness and of happiness which nature has scattered abroad, and expand them into maturity, and enrich them with fruit; should he be able to teach, to even a few of this generation, how mind is a god over matter; how in arranging objects of desire, a subordination of the less valuable to the more is the great secret of individual happiness; how the whole of life depends upon the scale which we form of its relative values,—could he do this, what diffusion, what intensity, what perpetuity of blessings he would confer! How would his beneficial influence upon mankind widen and deepen as it descended forever!

"I cannot think of that station as regards myself without feeling both hopes and fears, desires and apprehensions, multiplying in my mind,—so glorious a sphere, should it be crowned with success; so heavy with disappointment and humiliation, should it fail through any avoidable misfortune. What a thought, to have the future minds of such multitudes dependent in any perceptible degree upon one's own exertions! It is such a thought as must mightily energize or totally overpower any mind that can adequately comprehend it."

On May 27, 1837, the governor appointed eight gentlemen as the Board of Education. Mr. Mann was one of these. He believed this Board to be like a spring almost imperceptible, flowing from the highest tableland between oceans, destined to deepen and widen as it descended, diffusing health and beauty in its course till nations shall dwell upon its banks. He regarded this as the first great movement towards an organized system of common school education, which should be at once thorough and universal.

At this time he said,—"I would much sooner surrender a portion of the territory of the commonwealth to an ambitious and aggressive neighbor than I would surrender the minds of its children to the domain of ignorance."

On June 29, 1837, he was elected secretary of the Board of Education. Of the position and his relation to it, he says: "Few undertakings according to my appreciation of it have been greater. I know of none which may be more fruitful in beneficent results. God grant me an annihilation of selfishness, a mind of wisdom, a heart of benevolence! How many men I shall meet who are accessible only through a single motive, or who are incased in prejudice and jealousy, and need, not to be subdued but to be remodeled! how many who will vociferate their devotion to the public, but whose thoughts will be intent on themselves! There is but one spirit in which these impediments can be met with success: it is the spirit of self-abandonment, the spirit of martyrdom. To this I believe there are but few, of all who wear the form of humanity, who will not yield. I must not irritate, I must not humble, I must not degrade anyone in his own eyes. I must not present myself as a solid body to oppose an iron barrier to any. I must be a fluid sort of a man, adapting myself to tastes, opinions, habits, manners, so far as this can be done without hypocrisy or insincerity, or a compromise of principle. In all this there must be a higher object than to win personal esteem, or favor, or worldly applause. A new fountain may now be opened. Let me strive to direct its current in such a manner, that if, when I have departed from life, I may still be permitted to witness its course, I may behold it broadening and deepening in an everlasting progression of virtue and happiness.

"Henceforth, so long as I hold this office, I

devote myself to the supremest welfare of mankind upon earth. An inconceivably greater labor is undertaken. With the highest degree of prosperity, results will manifest themselves but slowly. The harvest is far distant from the seedtime. Faith is the only sustainer. I have faith in the improvability of the race,—in their accelerating improvability. This effort may do apparently but little. But mere beginning in a good cause is never little. If we can get this vast wheel into any perceptible motion, we shall have accomplished much. And more and higher qualities than mere labor and perseverance will be requisite. Art for applying will be no less necessary than science for combining and deducing. No object ever gave scope for higher powers, or exacted a more careful, sagacious use of them. At first, it will be better to err on the side of caution than of boldness. When walking over quagmires, we should never venture long steps. However, after all the advice which all the sages who ever lived could give there is no such security against danger, and in favor of success, as to undertake it with a right spirit,—with a self-sacrificing spirit. Men can resist the influence óf talent; they will deny demonstration, if need be; but few will combat goodness for any length of time. A spirit mildly devoting itself to a good cause is a certain conqueror. Love is a universal solvent. Wilfulness will maintain itself against persecution, torture, death, but will be fused and dissipated by any kindness, forbearance, sympathy. Here is a clew given by God to lead us through the labyrinth of the world."

Mr. Mann gave up the practice of law with no apparent regrets and wrote, almost with enthusiasm: "I have abandoned jurisprudence, and betaken myself to the larger sphere of mind and morals. Having found the present generation

composed of materials almost unmalleable, I am
about transferring my efforts to the next. Men
are cast-iron; but children are wax. Strength
expended upon the latter may be effectual, which
would make no impression upon the former."

"Let the next generation be my client," was
his call to duty as he turned from the courts to
the schools.

The spirit with which he entered upon this
work can have no better illustration than the
reply made to his friends who thought that the
office should have some better title than "secretary of the Board of Education," "If the title is
not sufficiently honorable now, then it is clearly
left for me to elevate it; and I would rather be
creditor than debtor to the title."

CHAPTER V.

It was a great task upon which Mr. Mann entered when he became secretary of the Massachusetts State Board of Education. There was never greater reverence for education in Massachusetts than at this time. The population was homogeneous; academies were numerous, and their inspiration was felt throughout the state. There was much home reading of good books, and every boy of any ambition worked out problems and studied by himself. Things were not as bad educationally as Mr. Mann thought them. There was fair teaching in every city and large town. The academies were enterprising. On a school diet of ten weeks a year Mr. Mann was a good illustration of what the home and school work was accomplishing. Massachusetts has never seen the time when she had a larger proportion of good scholars and grand men than when the Board of Education was organized. Whenever an enthusiast compares existing conditions with his ideals he finds the contrast between that which is and that which ought to be enough to exasperate a man of less zeal than himself. There has been no time in the history of Massachusetts, from the day of Peregrine White to this year in which the wife of the President of the United States invites a Boston kindergartner to apply all modern arts and devices to her daughter's education, in which there was a higher class of talent devoting its thought and energy to education or making greater sacrifices for the improvement of

childhood than in the decade in which Horace
Mann enlisted under the banner of the public
schools.

W. E. Channing, Theodore Parker, Samuel J.
May, Edward Everett, Governor Briggs, Josiah
Quincy, Robert Rantoul, Jr., Edmund Dwight,
James G. Carter and Cyrus Pierce were ready
to say and do all in their power for the good of the
schools. .What a surprise it would be to-day to
have the mayor of Boston give the secretary of the
Board of Education a check for $1,500 from his
own funds to be used in any way he saw fit for the
advancement of public school education, as his
grandfather Josiah Quincy, mayor of Boston, did
fifty-five years ago! What a sensation would be
created in the legislature were it announced that
some individual had made a donation of $10,000
for the professional training of teachers, as was
done less than sixty years ago by Edmund
Dwight. Jonathan Phillips, a private citizen, of
whom nothing else seems to be known, sent Mr.
Mann his check for $500 to use as he thought best
in the cause of public education. These conditions need to be understood in order that one may
appreciate the circumstances that led the president
of the Massachusetts senate to become the secretary of the Board of Education. The people as a
whole had no sympathy with the reformers who
were shouting long and loud about the degeneracy
of the times. Nor did Mr. Mann have any adequate
grounds for his early denunciation. Indeed he
had no thought of attacking any of the work or
workers of the day. All that actuated him might
well inspire any man in any age or in any community to make even greater sacrifices than those
which he proposed or experienced. It was not that
Mr. Mann wished to criticise the work done or to
antagonize the teachers in their work but he felt,
as who does not feel to-day, that America's future

depends upon the best common school education for those who need it most. His sympathies were always with the defective classes. He devoted much of his legislative energy to providing an asylum for the insane and educational advantages for the deaf, dumb and blind. This led him naturally, inevitably, to realize that many children had very little opportunity for school life, and that even the best teaching was far below the standard. It is as true now as it was then. The fact that he had but ten weeks in school in any year of his childhood inspired him to plan for something more and better for coming generations. "Let the next generation be my client" was his watchword.

Academies were much more influential then than now, and they were more efficient than the public schools. They had steadily gained since the close of the Revolutionary war. In 1780 there were few private schools, but in 1837, when Horace Mann began his work $328,000 was paid in one year as tuition in the academies and private schools of Massachusetts. This popularity of the academies was at the expense of the public schools in the wealthy communities. In 1837 the average expenditure per pupil in the state was $2.81 while in the twenty-nine most populous and wealthy towns it was but $2.21.

Enthusiasm for academies created the impression that the education of youth was of much greater moment than of children. In consequence little was done for children under ten years of age and in some communities nothing. Nantucket, then having 9,000 inhabitants, made no provision whatever for the younger or the older children but only for the grammar grade pupils.

There was almost no attempt to do anything at public expense for children of academic age. The educational ardor and aspiration therefore was tending more and more to benefit the few who would make some adequate return to the community in a scholastic way. There was no foreign population, and no parent allowed his children to grow up in ignorance. The home did much, the grammar school and the academy did more and the community was developing a good class of citizens.

Mr. Mann saw how important a part the churches played in the patronage of the academies, and his religious prejudices were aroused. He had honest doubts regarding the good accomplished by sectarian schools. He had high ideals of the good which must result from the education together of children of all classes. It was a blending of fear and hope combined with intense conviction that actuated him when he announced that his law library was for sale, bought such educational books as were to be found, and went to a quiet home at Franklin for a few days of study and meditation.

His special preparation for the work was not definite. He had seen little of schools as a pupil, had taught three short terms in rural schools, had instructed for a short time in college, had served for eight years on the school board of Dedham, had been closely associated with such inspiring work as the education of the deaf, dumb and blind, was the close friend of all the reformers in education from the outside but knew few teachers and had rarely attended educational gatherings. Maria Edgeworth and James Simpson were his most available authors.

Among the objects that he set himself to accomplish were the awakening of public sentiment through the holding of public educational gatherings, the introduction of school apparatus, the substituting of oral for text-book instruction, the training of teachers, the better construction of

schoolhouses, the use of better books, better ar-
rangement of studies, better modes of instruction.
He went into retirement at Franklin for a time
and prepared an address for the awakening of
public sentiment. When he began his career by
holding revival meetings in the interest of education in every village from Nantucket to Pittsfield,
he could not understand why people cared infinitely
more for a political speech than an educational
preachment, why they would leave him and go ten
miles to listen to a fourth-rate politician. In the
town of Barre, for illustration, the president of
the County Association and the president of the
American Institute of Instruction went twelve
miles to hear a political address when he was
lecturing upon education in their town. Of
Springfield, Mr. Mann wrote, "In point of numbers, a miserable meeting it has been." At Pittsfield there were only two or three people present.
At Worcester he said, "On the whole, I think a
little dent has been made in this place." After
speaking at Great Barrington, he wrote, "To make
an impression in Berkshire in regard to the
schools is like trying to batter down Gibraltar with
one's fist." After Northampton, he wrote, "Ah,
me! I have hold of so large a mountain that there
is much danger that I shall break my own back in
trying to lift it." Of Barnstable he wrote, "As
miserable a convention as can well be conceived.
I will work in this moral as well as physical sand-
bank of a county till I can get some new things
to grow out of it." Of Dedham, his old home
town, he says, "The convention was a meagre,
spiritless, discouraging affair. A few present
and all who were present chilled, choked by their
own fewness. If the schoolmaster is abroad in
this county I should like to meet him."

When Mr. Mann made a political speech at
Westport, a hundred people went over from New

Bedford to hear him, and the whole town turned out; but when, a few evenings later, he spoke in the same place on education, no one came from New Bedford, and scarcely any one came out at Westport. At Wellfleet he had "a miserable, contemptible, deplorable convention."

On a second visit to Pittsfield, he found that no arrangements had been made to prepare the schoolroom for the convention, so he and George N. Briggs, at that time governor of the state, purchased a broom and themselves swept the schoolhouse and put it in order. At ten o'clock, the time appointed for the convention, there was not an individual present. At 11.30 o'clock eight people had come. This is a sample of the "enthusiasm" with which his work was received. It was very annoying to him to feel that as a lawyer, politician and president of the senate he was a popular speaker, but that as an educator he could arouse little or no enthusiasm. Strange as this seems there have been many experiences of the officers of the Board of Education in recent years not unlike these of sixty years ago. Many meetings are held which are attended by almost none except teachers. In many towns already mentioned there have been educational gatherings with much talent provided at which the attendance was scandalously small. But Mr. Mann's enthusiasm did not wane, and he ultimately had the state thoroughly aroused. This was his great reward.

His new life was full of embarrassing incidents. The first Sunday that he was away from home on his new work was spent at Martha's Vineyard. There were three evangelical churches in Edgartown, a Congregational, Baptist and Methodist. Everyone knew that he was non-evangelical in his belief, and there was great curiosity to know at which of the churches he would worship; no one

had conceived the idea that he could avoid attend-
ing any. When the day arrived, to the consterna-
tion of all, he drove over to see the Chapoquiddie
Indians, with their guardian, Mr. Thaxter, who
wished his advice regarding the intellectual and
moral improvement of the tribe. He met the
Indians at the meeting-house-schoolhouse where
the Sunday school was held six months in the
year. This Sunday school was the only school
maintained for them, and this was for half the
year. This Sunday episode produced a scandal,
and the scene can be better imagined than described when a clergyman after riding nine miles
on Monday morning to attend the educational
meeting learned that the head of the educational
system of Massachusetts had been "to ride" instead of to church the previous day.

This work, however, was not without its en-
couragements. On November 10th of his first
year he went to Salem and held a convention during the day. He was booked also for an evening
lecture in the regular course of the city. The
convention was very thinly attended, even his
own personal friends, like Rantoul and Salton-
stall, not being present, but the few who were
there were so aroused by his address that they
insisted that it should be repeated as the lyceum
lecture of the evening, on which occasion the
popular response was so hearty as to cheer him
in his work for many a day. The first four years
were largely devoted to these crusades, to the
reading of the various school reports of the state,
and to writing his own state report. Greater devotion or faithfulness was never witnessed in any
school official.

CHAPTER VI.

THE NORMAL SCHOOLS.

The normal schools required much time and energy, sacrifice and wisdom. It was a great innovation that was proposed by James G. Carter, the most far-sighted man of that wonderful educational period. It was his thought first, his devotion and wisdom to the last, as it was Mr. Edmund Dwight's gift of $10,000 that made possible the first normal schools this side the sea, but to Mr. Mann the honor and the glory have been and ever will be given and rightly, too, although one may fail to explain the equity in such an assignment.

In 1647 Massachusetts took a position educationally that has been equaled by no other community on this continent when one considers its significance in point of time, conditions and projection through the subsequent two hundred and fifty years. The discussion as to the relative indebtedness of the colonists to England and the Netherlands has no place here,—suffice it to say that no community in either hemisphere has any such record of honor in education for so long a period as has Massachusetts since 1647. The methods have changed and the emphasis has been shifted from time to time, but it is one uninterrupted record of loyalty to education and of general progress. The apparent lapses are more in the seeming than in the fact.

Mr. Mann was never a historian; he had not the historian's instinct or training and his utterances upon the decadence of the system from 1647 to

1837 must be taken with several grains of allowance for his talent in special pleading. It is one of the requisites of a reformer to be able to magnify his own theory and practice, and to minify all that has preceded him. This vicious attitude toward other good workers is an indispensable virtue in any reformer. He must see only the weakness and wrong in the past and only strength and right in his own plans and purposes. John the Baptist's denunciations were vital to the love and mercy of Jesus. James G. Carter was more far-sighted and had greater wisdom in dealing with conditions; Edmund Dwight had more means and the consecration to use them, but neither had the heroism to say as did Horace Mann that from 1647 to 1826 the laws were altered again and again, to adapt them to the decreasing demands of the public in regard to schools.

There has been one pertinent illustration in modern times of the inevitable tendency to belittle one's predecessors in educational activity. The only real "reform" movement in education was twenty years ago when Quincy, Mass., attained a national reputation through Charles Francis Adams, Jr., who claimed to have reformed the schools of that town in his great pamphlet upon "The New Departure."

From 1852 to 1856 Charles Francis Adams, senior, was chairman of the school board of Quincy. The tone of his report was all that any reformer could ask. His administration was remarkably successful.

1852. "The standard of instruction has greatly risen, is rising yet. In no town has the advance been more marked than in Quincy. All the teachers for the past year are entitled to great credit.

1853. "The schools generally are in a very satisfactory condition. It is not too much to say of them that they will now compare with schools of

the same grade anywhere. Nowhere has the result been more satisfactory . . . highly satisfactory. . . . Highest approbation, etc.

1854. "The grammar school is now in all re-
spects in an excellent condition.

1855. "We have heard recitations in the high
school in French, in geometry, in algebra, in Latin
and in Greek which would have done credit to
any school in our commonwealth."

No more could have been said in praise of the
schools than is to be found on every page of the
reports written by Charles Francis Adams regarding the Quincy schools from 1852 to 1856.
Nor is it miscellaneous praise for the virtues are
discriminately set forth. He then resigned his
place to his son, John Quincy Adams, who was
chairman in 1857 and 59, 60 and 62, 70, 71, 72, 73.
Of the schools he wrote with the same enthusiasm
as his father had done.

1857. "The results are equal to the most sanguine expectations. There is not one of these
schools respecting which we would speak in terms
other than highest commendation.

1859. "The schools are a source of congratu-
lation and pride. . . . Schools are excellent. . . .
Method and manner with children is peculiarly
happy. Of the twenty-one schools in town not
one is bad . . . a feeling of general joy and surprise.

1860. "The results are highly satisfactory . . .
schools are good, most of them very good. It is
with hearty satisfaction that your committee can
honestly present so flattering a report.

1870. "The primary schools are in excellent
condition. The intermediate schools and their
teachers merit our highest commendation; they
are all good. The high school meets our highest
expectation."

In view of what is to be said by his brother

three years later the following is of special interest.

1871. "We have a custom of subjecting every school in town to a searching scrutiny by the whole committee at the close of the school year. This duty was performed with a good deal of thoroughness. All are excellent and all are improving."

Charles Francis Adams, Jr., a younger son, came upon the board the next year, 1872, and these schools that had been "highly satisfactory," "in excellent condition," "credit to any town in the commonwealth," "nothing better anywhere," "equal to the most sanguine expectations," "manner with children peculiarly happy," "examined with a searching scrutiny," "honestly present a flattering report," etc., etc., were found to have gone all to pieces for the accommodation of the third member of the same family Mr. Charles Francis Adams, Jr., who says:

1875. "This vain attempt to build upon nothing, costing the country untold millions of money . . . will surely lead us to mental bankruptcy if the stupendous fraud [so vigorously praised by father and brother] is not soon abolished and healthier plans and better teaching, etc. These methods [of his father and brother] turned scholars into parrots and made meaningless farce of education. For real results the teacher cared nothing. Smatter was the order of the day [under the system of his father and brother]. The teachers [of the father and brother] were old, lymphatic, listless schoolmarms. The examinations [of his father and brother] were a study for the humorist."

It does not require a humorist to enjoy the assurance with which this third member of the Adams family praises the results under his administration.

1875. "The application of these new ideas has produced as great a change in teaching as Har-

vey's great discovery did in medicine. The infant schools are transformed from painful to
pleasant places. The excellency or peculiarity
of our schools has excited a great deal of interest
among those persons who are observant of such
matters. The people of Quincy are gathering a
harvest of greater volume and value, etc. . . .
Really surprising progress has been effected in the
schools. . . . A high degree of excellency has
been attained where excellence is most unusual.
. . . We must frankly confess that we are in a
great measure satisfied with the work we are
doing, and have good reason to anticipate a constantly increasing improvement as we apply our
principles more thoroughly."

This chapter from modern history is introduced
merely to show that this tendency of human nature is very general and Mr. Mann must not be
censured for overdrawing the conditions of the
schools before he entered upon the work. The
bad is always indescribably bad, the good is never
extravagantly good, the indifference in unevent-
ful times is always heartrending to one who is
keenly alive to all the responsibilities of the hour.
It is equally true in political, social, educational
and religious life, and, until human nature
changes, it will continue to be so. Indifference can
be aroused and the best can triumph over the
worst only when someone possesses the masterly
power to make and meet a crisis. This power
Horace Mann possessed, and to him rather than
to any other man of his time belongs the honor
and the glory.

The normal schools introduced the modern im-
provements to the American schools. The academies which came in with the close of the Revolutionary war were to all intents and purposes the
normal schools for half a century. Nearly every
teacher in Massachusetts received his instruction

and inspiration at a New England academy. Too
much can hardly be said in their praise, but the
time came when they were thought to be possibilities for the rich alone. This fear was never fully
justified since the larger number in most of these
academies were poor boys "working their way,"
but for some cause the public schools in the
wealthier places were not universally patronized
by the "higher classes" of the community. There
was a final struggle between the inherited aristocratic sentiment from across the seas and the
new-born democracy of America.

Until the academy came, the sons of wealthy
people were largely educated in England. That
was the one aristocratic ideal. The academy was
the transition for the remnant of aristocracy to
the new democracy. It matters little whether or
not there was any justification for the fears enter-
tained from 1826 to 1837; the fact that these fears
existed necessitated a radical transformation to
uniform democracy in matters of education. It
was this transformation that Mr. Mann accomplished and the normal school is in large measure the instrumentality.

The first academy came at the close of the
French and Indian war (1763) through the gener-
osity of William Dummer, educated in the Boston Latin school and in the academies of England.
This was followed at the close of the Revolutionary war by Phillips Andover and Leicester
academies, and a score of other similar institutions. These furnished teachers for all the better
schools but they rapidly removed from the common schools all traces of Latin and Greek. In
1824 there were but seven towns in the state
required by law to provide for the teaching of
Latin. The teachers were very poorly qualified
for their work as soon as they were not required
to teach Latin. That requirement in the earlier

days had provided scholarly teachers. When that was abandoned the standard for men was ability to "fight it out" in the winter schools, and for women availability for the summer schools.

In 1824-5 James G. Carter of Lancaster wrote an earnest series of articles, over the signature "Franklin," for the Boston *Patriot*. His claim was that "the first step toward reform in our system of popular education, is the scientific preparation of teachers for the free schools. And the only measure that will insure to the public the attainment of this object, is to establish an institution for the very purpose."

At this time Horace Mann was beginning the practice of law in Dedham. Mr. Carter wrote upon·this theme with great ability for ten years before Mr. Mann's attention was given to the subject with any great devotion. To this agitation by Mr. Carter we owe the consecration of Mr. Mann, and we can readily understand the disappointment of Mr. Carter and the indignation of his friends when Mr. Mann was elected to the secretaryship which Mr. Carter had every reason to expect would come to him.

The first memorable act of the board was to recommend the passage of a law providing for the establishment of normal schools. In March, 1838. Hon. Edmund Dwight, one of the leading members of the board, offered through Mr. Mann $10,000 for the establishment of a normal school under the auspices of the state board, provided the Legislature would appropriate a similar sum. Within a month, April 19,—a date memorable from so many events,—the Legislature accepted the proposition. On May 30 the state board voted to establish a school in Plymouth county and December 28 it voted to locate two others at Lexington and Barre. The schools were opened, at Lexington July 3, 1839; at Barre, September 4,

1839; at Bridgewater, September 9, 1840. The
schools at Lexington and Barre were both removed so that Bridgewater is really the oldest
normal school on the continent. The location of
this school was due to the activity of Rev. Charles
Brooks of Hingham who had visited Prussia in
1835 and had steadily advocated the Prussian
system of professional training for Massachusetts. Thus really the normal schools were inspired by the Prussian system.

The first school opened was at Lexington under
the principalship of Cyrus Pierce, one of America's great teachers. At the opening only three
persons presented themselves for admission. It
grew slowly but steadily. Mr. Pierce did all the
teaching, superintended the interest of the board-
ing house, rose every morning in the winter at
3 o'clock to build the fires; a great part of the
time sleeping but three hours a night. The opening day to which Mr. Mann had looked forward
with bright anticipation proved to be one of the
most discouraging. He wrote of it, that night:
"What remains but more exertion, more and more,
till it must succeed." Two months later, on September 4th, the Barre school was opened with
twenty students. The governor of the commonwealth (George N. Briggs) opened the school with
a fine address upon the origin, progress, advantages and hopes of the normal school.

Mr. Mann gave much attention to these schools,
notably to the one at Lexington. He was greatly
annoyed at the criticisms which were heard on
every hand. In the nature of the case the talent
which applied for training was not always the
best; the course was all too brief; the equip-
ment too limited. There were many academies
that offered better opportunities for scholarship
and none of these institutions of learning were
friendly. The teachers already at work were in-

clined to interpret every argument for trained teachers as a reflection on themselves. Not every "normalite" succeeded as a teacher, in the judgment of the local authorities. The ideal normal was far removed from the real school and no one appreciated this more than Mr. Mann whose heart failed him many times in the first years of the schools.

Here are sample sentences from persons of educational influence: "Too much is claimed for the normal schools in their infant state." "The principals of the normal schools are comparatively inexperienced in public school-keeping. They are without that practice which makes perfect." "The experience of a graduate of a normal school, through the model school, is less than two weeks."

Mr. Mann was stimulated to greater effort and to higher endeavor because of these criticisms. He heard every word and used the judgment of his critics as his own instructor in perfecting these schools. The normal schools, now the glory of the educational work of America, owe more than will ever be expressed to his heroism, patience, devotion and skill.

CHAPTER VII.

OPPOSITION.

In the spring of 1840, the formal opposition to the Board of Education manifested itself. The *Observer,* the *Recorder* and some of the Boston dailies were making very bitter attacks upon the board, and in March, 1840, these assumed the proportion, as Mr. Mann said, of an "atrocious attack." He was fearful that the opposition would win in the Legislature. Referring to this possibility, he said: "This is bad. I must submit; but the cause shall not die if I can sustain or resuscitate it. New modes may be found if old ones fail. Perseverance, perseverance, and so on a thousand times and ten thousand times ten thousand." What a spirit! It was for such an hour that he had come into power.

His election was a great disappointment to James G. Carter and his friends. Mr. Carter had made the Board of Education and the normal schools a possibility; to him belonged the credit, to him should have gone the honor, had the question of honor been the first consideration. Hon. Edmund Dwight was not unappreciative of the service rendered by Mr. Carter, but he foresaw the emergencies that must arise and he was convinced that it was a question of service to a cause and not of honor to a man; and when the conflicts raged with such fury from March, 1840, to January, 1847, the wisdom of the choice was demonstrated. There was not another man in the state probably who could or would have led to victory as did Horace Mann.

Things were not as bad in the Legislature in
1840 as Mr. Mann feared, for the "bigots and van-
dals," as he styled them, were defeated by a vote
of 245 to 182. The author of this opposition movement was the next year dropped from the Legislature by his constituency "as a reward of his
malevolence." This was encouraging to Mr. Mann
who wrote, in the exuberance of victory: "The
common school is the institution which can receive and train up children in the elements of all
good knowledge and of virtue before they are
subjected to the alienating conceptions of life.
This institution is the greatest discovery ever
made by man; we repeat it, the common school is
the greatest discovery ever made by man. In two
grand characteristic attributes, it is supereminent
over all others; first in its universality, for it is capa-
cious enough to receive and cherish in its parental
bosom every child that comes into the world; and
second, in the timeliness of the aid it proffers,—
its early, seasonable supplies of counsel and guid-
ance making security antedate danger. Other
social organizations are curative and remedial;
this is a preventive and an antidote. They come
to heal diseases and wounds; this, to make the
physical and moral frame invulnerable to them.
Let the common school be expanded to its capa-
bilities, let it be worked with the efficiency of
which it is susceptible, and nine-tenths of the
crimes in the penal code will become obsolete; the
long catalogue of human ills will be abridged;
men will walk more safely by day; every pillow
will be more inviolable by night; property, life
and character will be held by a stronger tenure;
all rational hopes respecting the future will be
brightened."

But Mr. Mann's confidence in the Legislature's
disapproval of the opposition was not well placed,
for a minority of the Committee on Education

promptly reported a bill to transfer the powers
and duties of the Board of Education to the governor and council, and the duties of the secretary
to the secretary of state. This movement was
attributed with some justice to the radical evangelical members of the Legislature and caused
Mr. Mann no little anxiety, for the plea of economy
was very popular that year. The vote on the
measure was postponed from time to time through
the whole session, so that there was no peace for
the secretary, and he had little time or strength
to give to the legitimate work of the office. When
it did come to a vote, the opposition chose an hour
when everything was to its advantage, but even
then the board was sustained by a vote of 131 to
114. Of this Mr. Mann wrote to a friend: "Never
was any question taken under circumstances more
disadvantageous to the prevailing party, and I
am inclined to think that it will be considered, in
flash language, a settler."

The next year, 1842, the opposition made no
demonstration in the Legislature and the feeling
was very strong towards the board and its meas-
ures. Mr. Mann secured an appropriation of
$6,000 a year for three years for the normal
schools and $15 for each school district in the
state for a school library, on condition of its rais-
ing a like amount. These annual legislative afflic-
tions were more venomous and terrific than one
in this day can appreciate. Religious opposition
to Mr. Mann and his work was very keen; the
anti-temperance sentiment was ever on the alert
to discomfort him, the proslavery forces were
always against him, and all phases of conserva-
tism made him a target. Combined with all these
was a bitter opposition from the teachers and the
ever ready plea for economy. Mr. Mann met every
issue and every foe and won in every conflict. He
had more medals of victory than ever came to any

other educator. What Patrick Henry was in 1765, Sam Adams in 1775 and Abraham Lincoln in 1856-60, Horace Mann was in 1840-47. Men are raised up for special work and no man ever came to the kingdom in better time than Horace Mann, the educator.

CHAPTER VIII.

To his annual reports Mr. Mann gave his best thought. There have been no such official educational documents prepared in any country. The later reports of the Massachusetts board, its secretary and agents have often been of inestimable value. Superintendent W. T. Harris of St. Louis, Superintendent Henry F. Harrington of New Bedford, Superintendent George Howland of Chicago, and others, issued great reports but there has been nothing to compare with these twelve reports of Mr. Mann. The state of New York reprinted one of them entire, distributing 18,000 copies gratis through the state. At least one of them was republished entire at public expense in England and one at least was translated and republished entire at government expense in Germany. Parliament invited him to enlarge upon that department of his seventh report which referred to the schools of Great Britain and reprinted it as a government document.

Many of his public addresses were printed and extensively circulated. His address before the American Institute of Instruction at New Bedford, August, 1842, was specially published in an edition of 20,000 for free distribution. There has never been anything to compare with the volume of his writing, its freshness and vigor, its practical and philosophical wisdom. At this day it is a better education to read his twelve reports, his speeches and his controversies than the writings of any ten men aside from Henry Barnard and W. T. Harris. His first annual report (1837) must have been a revelation in that day as it is without a peer even to this day. He said: "The object of the common school system is to give to every child a free, straight, solid pathway, by which he can walk directly up from the ignorance of an infant to a knowledge of the primary duties of a man." He devotes the report to an exhaustive, scholarly, mighty treatment of these questions: The situation, construction, condition and number of schoolhouses; the manner in which school committee-men discharge their duties; the interest felt by the community in the education of all its children; the position in which a certain portion of the community stands in relation to free schools; the competency of teachers. Upon each of these he enlarged with much brilliancy, discussing every phase of these questions.

His argument for expert supervision was as skilful and vigorous as anything uttered in later times: "The state employs in the common schools more than three thousand teachers at an expense of more than $465,000 raised by direct taxation. But they have not one-thousandth part of the supervision which watches the same number of persons having the care of cattle, spindles or of the retail of shop goods. Who would retain his reputation for sanity, if he employed men on his farm, or in his factory month after month without oversight and even without inquiry." In this tone he sweeps on from point to point with marvelous power.

The second annual report (1838) was largely an arraignment of the educational means and methods as he found them. The first had treated of ideals and their attainment as applied to education in the state. In the second he showed that "the common school system of Massachusetts had fallen into a state of general unsoundness and de-

bility." The schoolhouses were ill adapted to en-
courage mental effort and absolutely perilous to
the health of children; the schools were under
sleepy supervision; many of the most intelligent
and wealthy citizens had become estranged from
their welfare, and the teachers, although, with very
few exceptions, persons of estimable character
and of great private worth, yet in the absence of
all opportunity to qualify themselves for the performance of the most difficult and delicate task
committed to human hands, were deeply and widely
deficient in a knowledge of the human mind as the
subject of improvement and a knowledge of the
means best adapted wisely to unfold and direct
its growing faculties. "To expect that a system
animated only by a feeble principle of life, and
that life of irregular action, could be restored at
once to health and vigor, would be a sure preparation for disappointment."

There has never been a more close, scientific
study of the actual conditions than those which
led to the publication of this second report. This
analytic study is supplemented by a remarkable
presentation of pedagogical principles. He shows
that in learning the effective labor must be performed by the learner himself and generally this
must be a conscious effort on the part of the pupil,
who must not be a passive recipient but an active,
voluntary agent. He must do more than admit
or welcome, he must reach out, and grasp, and
bring home. The teacher must bring knowledge
within arm's length of the learner; must break
down its masses into portions so minute, that they
can be taken up and appropriated one by one, but
the final appropriating act must be learner's.
Knowledge is not annexed to the mind but the mind
assimilates it by its own vital powers. Each must
earn his own knowledge by the labor of his own
brain. Nature recognizes no title to learning by

inheritance, gift or finding. Development of mind is ·by growth and organization. All effective teaching must have reference to this indispensable, consummating act and effort of the learner. Every scholar in the school must think with his own mind as every singer in the choir must sing with her own voice. The first requisite is the existence in the mind of a desire to learn. Children who spend six months in learning the alphabet will, on the playground in a single half-day or moonlight evening, learn the intricacies of a game or sport,—where to stand, where to run, what to say, how to count, and what are the laws and the ethics of the game; the whole requiring more intellectual effort than would suffice to learn half a dozen alphabets. So of the recitation of verses, mingled with action, and of juvenile games, played in the chimney corner. And the reason is, that for the one, there is desire; while against the other, there is repugnance. The teacher, in one case, is rolling weight up hill, in the other down; for gravitation is not more to the motions of a heavy body than desire is to the efficiency of the intellect. Until a desire to learn exists within the child, some foreign force must constantly be supplied to keep him going; but from the moment that a desire is excited, he is self-motive and goes alone.

As is often the case, the multitude of virtues in this report made much less impression than the few stinging sentences, as "sleepy supervision," "a state of general unsoundness and debility," "animated only by a feeble principle of life and that life in irregular action." The wide world over his great utterances were appreciated but at home the few sharp expressions rankled and were never forgotten by the leading teachers.

The third annual report (1839) dealt with the people and their responsibility for the improve-

ment of the schools. It also dwelt upon the ne-
cessity of public libraries for the general intelligence and upon universal and ever enlarging educational opportunities. The characteristic feature of Mr. Mann's reports is the way in which he
grapples with one or two subjects and treats them
with the mastery of a statesman. In this third
report he shifts the responsibility largely from
the teacher to the community, to public sentiment, to liberality of support, to loyalty to the
highest good in locating school buildings, choos-
ing and retaining teachers. His treatment of the
factory question in relation to attendance should
be reprinted and circulated in the factory towns
all over the land.

After portraying the educational effect of having a child become a part of a machine by the
regularity of his movements according to orders
in a factory, he draws this terrible indictment of
the system.

"The ordinary movements of society may go
on without any shocks or collisions; as, in the human system, a disease may work at the vitals,
and gain a fatal ascendancy there, before it mani-
fests itself on the surface. But the punishment
for such an offence will not be remitted because
its infliction is postponed. The retribution, indeed, is not postponed, it only awaits the full
completion of the offence; for this is a crime of
such magnitude, that it requires years for the
criminal to perpetrate it in, and to finish it off
thoroughly in all its parts. But when the children
pass from the conditions of restraint to that of
freedom, from years of enforced but impatient
servitude to that independence for which they
have secretly pined, and to which they have looked
forward, not merely as the period of emancipa-
tion, but of long-delayed indulgence; when they
become strong in the passions and propensities

that grow up spontaneously, but are weak in the moral powers that control them, and blind in the intellect which foresees their tendencies; when, according to the course of our political institutions, they go, by one bound, from the political nothingness of a child to the political sovereignty of a man,—then, for that people who so cruelly neglected and injured them, there will assuredly come a day of retribution."

The public libraries of Massachusetts are her pride as they are the wonder and admiration of the world, and for them we are largely indebted to this third annual report of Mr. Mann. For all true, wise advocates of public libraries will turn to this treasure-house of argument for their inspiration.

The fourth annual report grappled with the great educational vice of the century following the Revolution, the local school district, which George H. Martin has so aptly characterized as "the high-water mark of modern democracy and the low-water mark of the Massachusetts school system." Mr. Mann attempted to remedy this by the union of districts. It is in this fourth report that he deals with greatest vigor with the problems presented by the normal schools.

It is interesting to note, at this time, when the universities are very generally succeeding in the introduction into the grammar schools of "university studies," and demanding "university flavor" for the normal schools, that Mr. Mann always felt that one of the great victories of his educational career was the exclusion of pretension to scholarship and the accomplishment of thoroughness in the branches a knowledge of which was fundamental.

"At the normal school at Barre during the last term, the number of pupils was about fifty. This number might have been doubled if the visitors

would have consented to carry the applicants
forward at once into algebra and chemistry and
geometry and astronomy, instead of subjecting
them to a thorough review of common-school
studies. One of the most cheering auguries in
regard to our schools is the unanimity with which
the committees have awarded sentence of condemnation against the practice of introducing
into them the studies of the university to the exclusion or neglect of the rudimental branches.
By such a practice a pupil foregoes all the stock
of real knowledge he might otherwise acquire;
and he receives in its stead only a show or coun-
terfeit of knowledge, which, with all intelligent
persons, only renders his ignorance more con-
spicuous. A child's limbs are as well fitted in
point of strength to play with the planets before
he can toss a ball, as his mind is to get any conception of the laws which govern their stupendous
motions before he is master of common arithmetic. For these and similar considerations, it
seems that the first intellectual qualification of a
teacher is a critical thoroughness, both in rules
and principles, in regard to all the branches required by law to be taught in the common schools;
and a power of recalling them in any of their parts
with a promptitude and certainty hardly inferior
to that with which he could tell his own name."

This fourth report may be characterized as
high-water mark in the practical treatment of
every-day questions connected with education.

The fifth annual report was the first to create
a sensation the world over. There had been a
growing reverence for the man throughout America and in foreign parts but it was this fifth report
(1841) that was printed at public expense and dis-
tributed by the tens of thousand copies by the
New York legislature, by British authorities, and
by the German government. It is a glorious

presentation of the effect of education upon 'the worldly fortunes of men,—upon property, upon human comfort and competence, upon the outward, visible, material interests or well-being of individuals and communities. He showed that the aggregate wealth of a town will be increased just in proportion to the increase of its appropriations for schools; tax for schools is an investment and not a burden; money invested in the education of a child will more than double his patrimony. Education ministers to our personal and material wants beyond all other agencies, whether excellence of climate, spontaneity of production, mineral resources, or mines of silver and gold.

He shows the difference in productive ability between the educated and the uneducated, "between a man or woman whose mind has been awakened to thought and supplied with the rudiments of knowledge by a good common-school education and one whose faculties have never been developed, or aided in emerging from their original darkness and torpor, by such a privilege."

The effect of this report was not to glorify the material aspect for he says: "This tribute is still the faintest note of praise that can be uttered in honor of so noble a theme; and however deserving of attention may be the economical view of the subject yet it is one that dwindles into insignificance when compared with these loftier and more sacred attributes of the cause which have the power of converting material wealth into spiritual well-being, and of giving to its possessor lordship and sovereignty alike over the temptations of adversity, and the still more dangerous seducements of prosperity, and which—so far as human agency is concerned—must be looked to for the establishment of peace and righteousness upon earth, and for the enjoyment of glory and happiness in heaven."

The sixth annual report (1842) attracted comparatively little attention dealing as it did largely
with the question of teaching physiology in
schools. Mr. Mann was very generally suspected
of coming dangerously near being a "crank," and
his work had been hindered in many important
phases by this malarial suspicion. He was radical on the temperance question, was an intense
enthusiast over the insane, the deaf, dumb and
blind, and was withal an ardent champion of
phrenology. These facts, taken as a whole, led
the great body of the people to fear that sooner
or later he would go off at a tangent, so that when
this sixth report appeared, one of the longest he
had written, devoted largely to physiology they
accepted without hesitation the general judgment
that the expected had happened. For six years
he had had many very bitter opponents, but the
more influential among them had nursed their
wrath in silence. There had been an element of
devotion and of grandeur in the first five reports
that led such men to say "the hour has not struck"
for us to speak. This sixth report came also at a
time when public impatience with phrenology
was quite distinct so that the appearance of this
report marked the moment of misfortune for Mr.
Mann. He had done the wrong thing at the
wrong time and no one realized this more than he.
These conditions must be taken into account in
estimating the great controversy with the "Thirty-
one Boston Masters" which followed. Mr. Mann
thought he was doing the best thing possible to
right his craft when he married and went abroad
for several months. The former act was a bless-
ing for which he never ceased to be thankful, but
the trip abroad was the beginning of fateful com-
plications.

CHAPTER IX.

THE FAMOUS SEVENTH REPORT.

A sad chapter in Mr. Mann's life is that which deals with his controversy with the thirty-one Boston masters. Had he died with the issuance of his fifth annual report he would have been glorified in death as at no other hour of his life. Had he "passed away" when he sailed for Europe, there would have been a host of good people in Massachusetts to say: "Well, he dies at a good time." But his permanent place in educational history is due to the great controversy with the Boston masters more than to all other experiences of his life. In its humiliation which was great, appeared his ultimate power. There was never a better illustration of the truth that emergencies make men.

His fifth report was the climax of his growing power; its reception by all peoples of both hemispheres threw him off his guard. He was physically worn out and mentally exhausted. The highest aspirations of his professional life seemed about to be realized and he wrote this report on physiology, which, though a great document in itself, came as an anti-climax to an expectant people.

From the first his standard had been the Prussian schools which had in twenty years attained ideal conditions, consequently when he went abroad he studied those schools as a worshipper. He was lionized everywhere in Scotland, England, Ireland, Germany, Saxony, Holland, Belgium, France and Prussia. His fifth report met him in every land and he returned with renewed physical and mental vigor, with higher aspirations, and a realization of the fact that he was no longer merely the secretary of the Massachusetts State Board of Education, but an international educational leader. He wrote his famous seventh annual report (1843) with every condition favorable for the highest flights but equally so for occasional descents. No man ever had occasion to expect more from any official utterance than Mr. Mann from this report, both hemispheres were awaiting it and he had every reason to anticipate a chorus of praise.

This seventh report was almost exclusively concerned with what he saw abroad. Read in the light of modern times when criticism is freely indulged in, one cannot understand why any special exception should have been taken to this report in which he said: "I have visited countries where there is no national system of education, and countries where the minutest details of the schools are regulated by law. I have seen schools in which each word and process, in many lessons, was almost overloaded with explanations and commentary; and many schools in which four or five hundred children were obliged to commit to memory in the Latin language, the entire book of Psalms and other parts of the Bible, neither teachers nor children understanding a word of the language which they were prating. I have seen countries in whose schools all forms of corporal punishment were used without stint or measure; and I have visited one nation in whose excellent and well-ordered schools scarcely a blow has been struck for more than a quarter of a century. On reflection, it seems to me that it would be most strange if, from all this variety of system and of no system, of sound instruction and of babbling, of the discipline of violence and of

moral means, many beneficial hints for our warn-
ing or our imitation could not be derived."

To a reader of our day, he appears to have
written in the best of spirit, though he says: "I
do not hesitate to say that there are many things
abroad which we, at home, should do well to imi-
tate; things, some of which are here, as yet, mere
matters of speculation and theory, but which,
there, have long been in operation, and are now
producing a harvest of rich and abundant blessings. If the Prussian schoolmaster has better
methods of teaching reading, writing, grammar,
geography, arithmetic, etc., so that, in half the
time, he produces greater and better results,
surely we may copy his modes of teaching these
elements, without adopting his notions of passive
obedience to government, or of blind adherence
to the articles of a church. By the ordinance of
nature, the human faculties are substantially the
same all over the world; and hence the best means
for their development and growth in one place
must be substantially the best for their development and growth everywhere. The spirit which
shall control the action of these faculties when
matured, which shall train them to self-reliance
or to abject submission, which shall lead them to
refer all questions to the standard of reason, or
to that of authority,—this spirit is wholly distinct and distinguishable from the manner in
which the faculties themselves should be trained;
and we may avail ourselves of all improved methods in the earlier processes, without being con-
taminated by the abuses which may be made to
follow them. The best style of teaching arithmetic or spelling has no necessary or natural connection with the doctrine of hereditary right; and
an accomplished lesson in geography or grammar
commits the human intellect to no particular dog-
ma in religion.

"A generous and impartial mind does not ask whence a thing comes, but rather 'what is it?' Those who at the present day, would reject an improvement because of the place of its origin, belong to the same school of bigotry with those who inquired if any good could come out of Nazareth; and what infinite blessings would the world have lost had that party been punished by success! Throughout my whole tour, no one principle has been more frequently exemplified than this—that wherever I have found the best institutions,—educational, reformatory, charitable, penal or otherwise,—there I have always found the greatest desire to know how similar institutions were administered among ourselves; and where I have found the worst, there I have found most of the spirit of self-complacency, and even an offensive disinclination to hear of better methods."

He takes occasion to speak with exuberant praise of the work done by his friend, Dr. S. G. Howe in the Institution for the Blind. He gives an elaborate transcript of the lesson he heard taught in a Scotch school, but his greatest enthusiasm is manifest in his description of work in the Prussian schools, emphasizing their methods of teaching reading. Referring to these schools, he says that he is persuaded that no thorough reform will be effected in Massachusetts schools till the practice of beginning with the alphabet is abolished, and says when he inquired in Prussia if they began with the names of the letters as given in the alphabet, the look they gave him implied no great respect for his professional intelligence. He devotes several pages to ridiculing the alphabet method. He thus considers each of the elementary school subjects.

This report appeared in the spring and was immediately construed by the Boston masters as a reflection upon their methods. The first reception of the report was the most enthusiastic given to any of his publications, but the private criticism greatly annoyed him, and he wrote, as early as April, "There are owls who to adapt the world to their own eyes would always keep the sun from rising. Most teachers amongst us have been animated to greater exertions by the account of the best schools abroad. Others are offended at being driven out of the paradise which their own self-esteem had erected for them." The first open attack was through the columns of a religious paper. These attacks became very virulent and Mr. Mann replied; but in publishing his reply the editor made some "weak and wicked" comments, to which he also replied. This reply was not published in that paper but printed elsewhere, and a lively newspaper controversy followed.

CHAPTER X.

Through the spring and summer, in nearly every educational convention held throughout the state, some of the grammar masters of Boston, Worcester and other cities were sure to be upon the program and always with an attack on the ideas presented by Mr. Mann in his seventh annual report. But all this, though annoying, was unimportant in comparison with "The Remarks on the Seventh Annual Report of the Hon. Horace Mann," a document of 144 pages issued by the thirty-one Boston masters. These "Remarks" were prepared by four different members of the Masters' Association, each section read before that body, and then published in the hope that they might "help in some degree to correct erroneous views and impressions, and thus tend to promote a healthy tone in public sentiment in relation to many things connected with the welfare of our common schools." "The teacher, who has stood for many years, himself against a host of five or six hundred children from all ranks and conditions of society, thinks he may once ask a hearing before the public. We know that literary and moral amateurs seem very often to repudiate the notion, that 'experience is the best schoolmaster.' We would not less eschew impatience with such and the great community, than with the children of our charge. We desire no assent to anything which is not right and reasonable; but being of one mind in regard to great cardinal principles, we shall once, at least, venture 'abroad' in their defence."

The thirty-one masters who signed this document were: Barnum Field, Franklin School; Joseph Hale, Johnson School; Samuel S. Greene, New North School; Cornelius Walker, Wells School; William D. Swan, Mayhew School; William A. Shepard, Brimmer School; A. Andrews, Bowdoin School; James Robinson, Bowdoin School; William J. Adams, Hancock School; Peter Mackintosh, Jr., Hancock School; Samuel Barrett, Adams School; Josiah Fairbank, Adams School; C. B. Sherman, Eliot School; Levi Conant, Eliot School; Aaron D. Capen, Mayhew School; Frederick Crafts, Hawes School; John Alex. Harris, Hawes School; Abner Forbes, Smith School; Albert Bowker, Lyman School; Nathan Merrill, Franklin School; Reuben Swan, Jr., Wells School; George Allen, Jr., Endicott School; Loring Lathrop, Endicott School; Henry Williams, Jr., Winthrop School; Samuel L. Gould, Winthrop School; Thomas Baker, Boylston School; Charles Kimball, Boylston School; Joshua Bates, Jr., Brimmer School; Benj. Drew, Jr., New North School; J. A. Stearns, Mather School; Jona. Battles, Jr., Mather School.

These "Remarks" were as brilliant productions as ever came from the pens of grammar masters. Six months, practically, had been spent in the preparation. Of course there is much which now seems too ridiculous to have been written with seriousness which then passed for brilliant appeals to the convictions and prejudices of the people. The masters make a strong presentation of the virtues of the "Puritan fathers who founded a university in ten years after they landed upon New England's rude and rocky shore," and established the common schools—"to whose influence the present generation is in-

debted for most of the civic, social and religious
blessings"; call attention to the fact that the
great leaders of two hundred years could boast
no higher alma mater than the rude room of some
humble house in which they gathered a few weeks
each season; and seem to apologize for the
teachers "who have left behind them monuments
which should exact feelings of gratitude rather
than produce dissatisfaction."

"With all the rude fixtures and other inconven-
iences for school purposes, an enlightened public
sentiment was early formed, which sustained the
State Legislature in giving hundreds of thousands
of dollars to the colleges and other seminaries of
learning. After making allowance for the social
evils of war and intemperance, the progress of
education to the present time seems truly wonderful. The good cause was never more prosper-
ous than at the time the Board of Education was
formed, and the establishment of such a body,
with little or no opposition, certainly indicated a
healthy tone in public sentiment. All the friends
of the common schools from the governor to the
most humble citizen, felt a desire to see these
institutions improved, and their blessings extended to every child in the commonwealth. The
desire was for improvement, and not for revolution, in that 'ancient and cherished institution, the
common schools of Massachusetts.'" Mr. Mann
had described a performance by the blind on
organs unusual in this country, organs construc-
ted with a set of keys for the feet, so that the feet
could play an accompaniment to the hands, and
he is informed, sarcastically, that there are fifty
such organs in churches within sight of the State
House. Mr. Mann claimed that in six weeks he
visited hundreds of schools and saw tens of thousands of scholars, saying that he did not merely
look at these schools but that he entered them

before the first recitation in the morning and remained until after the last at night. He is reminded that in another connection he speaks facetiously of the mathematical instruction in our schools saying, "If a boy states that he has seen 10,000 horses and you make him count 10,000 kernels of corn, he will never see so many horses again," and they suggest that if he should count the number of school days in six weeks he would not visit so many hundreds of schools or see so many tens of thousands of scholars in the same time.

Mr. Mann commends the good conduct in the Holland schools where they have no corporal punishment, remarking that one pupil in 100 is expelled for bad conduct. His attention is called to the fact that good conduct is rather expensive according to his own showing.

"A sacrilegious hand has been laid upon everything mental, literary and moral that did not conform to the new light of the day. Fulminations of sarcasm and ridicule, from the lecture room and the press, in essays and speeches, were the forebodings of the new era in the history of common schools, and in the experience of teachers. After Washington had crossed the Delaware, in the darkest hour of the Revolution, Congress gave him new power, in consideration of the new work before him; but it seemed that before the teacher could be allowed to go on in his great work of warring against ignorance, idleness and vice, his authority should be abridged, and all his acquired reputation and influence forfeited, as would be the goods of a contraband trade. All exaggerated accounts of cases in the school discipline of some teachers, and the supposed disqualifications of others, seemed to be set forth to lessen the authority, influence and usefulness of teachers, and give a new direction to public sentiment.

"In matters of education, how vain and worthless have been spasmodic efforts and hot-béd theories, in which the projectors have disregarded expense and observation! Of such vagaries, in the first place, may be mentioned the infant school system, which, for a while was the lion of its day. The fond parent, the philosopher, and the philanthropist, were equally captivated by the scintillations of infantile genius. The doting mother and the credulous aunt, with rapturous delight told their friends of the rapid progress of the prattling child; and the learned president of a New England college, when he heard the little philosopher say that the hat, including the ribbon and buckle, was composed of parts of the three kingdoms of nature, the animal, vegetable and mineral, remarked that he then saw by what means the world would be converted; and he seemed to think that in Geology, Botany, and Zoology, there would be no farther need of the services of Lyell, Gray and Audubon; but the object of live mental vision proved an ignis fatuus. The sister of a distinguished governor said the whole affair of infant schools reminded her of those youthful days when she planted beans in the garden and soon pulled them up to see if the roots had grown."

The normal schools, in their early days afforded abundant opportunity for these critics to turn against them many of the things that Mr. Mann had said regarding the common school system.

Mr. Mann's reason for going abroad was the fact that he had spent six years and spared neither labor nor expense in fulfilling that portion of the law which requires that the secretary shall collect information; and for this purpose had visited schools in most of the free states and in several of the slave states of the Union, and had done all he could to learn what was being accom-

plished throughout this country. He had turned
his eyes again and again to some new quarter of
the horizon with the hope that they might be
greeted by a brighter beam of light.

"Actual observation alone can give anything
approaching to the true idea. I do not exag-
gerate when I say that the most active and lively
schools I have ever seen in the United States
must be regarded almost as dormitories, if compared with the fervid life of the Scotch schools;
and, by the side of theirs, our pupils would seem
to be hibernating animals just emerging from
their torpid state, and as yet but half conscious
of the possession of life and faculties. It is
certainly within bounds to say there were six
times as many questions put and answers given,
in the same space of time, as I ever heard put
and given in any school in our own country."

"Nor is this all. The teacher does not stand
immovably fixed to one spot (I never saw a
teacher in Scotland sitting in a school-room), nor
are the bodies of the pupils mere blocks, resting
motionless in their seats, or lolling from side to
side as though life were deserting them."

Mr. Mann is asked what he knows of the present
state of the Boston schools from actual observation and is told that he knows comparatively
nothing as he has not in six years visited a single
school in the city and knows nothing of them by
observation and he makes hasty statements and
comparisons upon matters abroad and at home.
For instance, he devotes a chapter to music in the
Prussian schools while he never heard any singing exercise in the Boston schools. It is not
known to any of the masters that the secretary
has improved any opportunity, within five years,
of knowing anything of the views of Boston
teachers or anything of their plans or the result
of their instruction. He has not held a meeting

in Boston for six years, and it is difficult for us to
understand how Mr. Mann could have collected
or diffused any information in Suffolk County.
Many of the thirty-one masters were graduates
of colleges and universities, had had much experience, frequently assembling themselves together,
and had delivered addresses upon many educational subjects.

All in all, this was a bright, strong document
with which the thirty-one masters might well feel
satisfied, but the times were against them. Five
years before, this would have been a stunning
blow, but the sentiment had changed, and though
they were congratulated by the fraternity, it
rallied to the support of Mr. Mann multitudes who
had hesitated hitherto to identify themselves
with him. Though many laughed at the sharp
thrusts and the just criticisms, they ended by
sympathizing with him, saying that he would
be more careful of his rhetoric and his figures
another time. Although it was rumored for
some weeks that the Boston masters were plan-
ning a severe attack on Mr. Mann he was taken
entirely by surprise. He had no suspicion that
his report was so vulnerable nor that the masters
were so able. Six months of close study were
given to their work and when it appeared it was
a masterpiece. The effect upon Mr. Mann was all
and more than his bitterest opponent could ask.
It cut him to the quick. Speaking of it to a friend
in England he said that he had suffered severely
in the conflict so far as his feelings were concerned and added, "I have doubtless suffered con-
siderably in reputation." He was severely
wrenched by their criticisms and replied while
his indignation had the better of his judgment.

CHAPTER XI.

Up to this time every public utterance had been prepared with the utmost care, with a view to permanence in literature, universal scholarly respect, and the highest influence. Now he forgot all this and wrote without preparation, and with a feeling of contempt for his antagonists. In this last phase of mind lay his greatest weakness. Notwithstanding his effort in the "Reply" to give the impression that he had the highest respect for teachers—some teachers—one cannot escape the feeling that he had never had any adequate respect for the Boston masters. He estimated them by their numbers, their influence gained through the other teachers who were indebted to them, and through their pupils whose loyalty was natural. In a letter written at the time may be seen his misconception of the men, affirming, as he does, that these grammar school masters saw their own condemnation in these descriptions of their European contemporaries, and "resolved as a matter of self-preservation, to keep out the infection of so fatal an example as was afforded by the Prussian schools"; the spirit of evil prevailed among the masters; the writing of the "Remarks" fell into bad hands. The same spirit appears when he says that the normal school at Lexington was so much above even the conception of most teachers as not to be appreciated by them as a rule.

When these "Remarks" appeared he would not acknowledge their ability or the strength of any of their positions, but applied ridicule and treated them largely with contempt. It is easy to see how he could have crushed the masters at a single blow had he dealt with them after his usually careful and artistic fashion in a pamphlet of twenty pages; instead, he chose to write 175 pages, many of which were in no sense creditable to him.

He read their "Remarks" with astonishment and grief but proceeded to show very clearly that indignation and retaliation played a more important part. They were accused of introducing his name a hundred times and more in connection with sentiments that he never felt and with expressions that he never uttered; they were not philosophical but censorious and aspersive; many of them were young, "mewling and purling in their nurses' arms" when the principals of the normal schools had achieved success; the grammar masters were "like thirty-one vulgar fractions multiplied into themselves, yielding a most contemptible product"; there were "sutures and overlappings where the heterogeneous parts are rudely joined together"; they showed a "culpable indifference to truth and the sacredness of character"; their literary effort as claimed by themselves in the "Remarks" would have required but a line a day from each in the time devoted to it; many of the "Remarks" were old lectures new-vamped; it must have been remorseless imposition of labor; the pages swam with error.

The depth of his feeling is best shown when at the close of a long plea for harmony between himself and the thirty-one masters, he makes an exception in regard to one individual, the "author whoever he may be of the first section as far as page 38" saying, "until he changes his nature or I change my nature we must continue to dwell on opposite sides of the moral universe." He then devotes more than a page to his characterization

of this "maligner." Some of the signatures affected
him with amazement and unspeakable regret and
could tears of night efface them, they would be
gladly shed. His report had been mutilated and
garbled; the shade had been copied and all the
light omitted; a forgery of the original had been
sent out; they had made fraudulent transposi-
tions.

The "Reply" was certainly earnest and the
writer had all the over-confidence of an accused
man who knows his innocence and knows that he
can prove it, but it is inconceivable that a man of
his talent and experience should recite the fact
that he had taught district schools, tutored in
college and served on a country school board as
though these were any adequate training. It was
the man and not his trifling previous experience
in school work that led to his call to the secretaryship. He nowhere appears to less advantage
than when he meets their arraignment for not
having visited the Boston schools. It is inconceivable that he should give pages to the
proof that it was not possible for them to know
absolutely of their own experience whether or not
he had visited the schools, since some of them had
not been teaching in their present positions so
long and they were not always in attendance; and
proceed to charge them with bearing false witness in testifying that they knew what they could
not have known; giving much space to showing
that he had once heard a singing lesson, had
visited two schools with the mayor spending
half an hour in each, had been at an exhibition
and in all had visited the Boston schools twelve
times in five years and then try to demonstrate
that this is their mathematical share of his time.
It was fruitless, also, for him to attempt to escape the responsibility for having spoken dis-
paragingly of teachers by citing pages of fairly

complimentary things said of them in other reports and addresses. No one knew better than Mr. Mann that there can be no trial balance in such cases, that there are debts that can never be paid off in that way. A man may have paid millions in the past but it does not save him from insolvency when the last great debt appears in judgment. It was equally useless for a man in his position to seek exemption from the consequences of his undervaluation by quoting from other lesser men who had spoken with greater indiscretion. There was not wanting abundance of opportunity for a terrific blow had he been in the mood and condition to have dealt it. Their claim that the schools of the Commonwealth were in excellent condition when he came into office is met in a masterly manner; in many towns education was sadly neglected; there was no provision for higher education at public expense except in a few cities; there was in many places no provision for children under nine or ten; many schools were open but a few weeks; and many scholars travelled from one section of the town to another. In this their charge was skilfully met.

The assumption that he had in any wise attacked the Boston schools was almost cruelly met with the cold facts that he had merely mentioned Boston with Lexington and a few other places in Massachusetts to show the relative location compared with the places visited in Europe, and that the attempt to make him connect Boston with the Scotch schools was more than absurd, it was vicious. There is no gainsaying his accusation that their method of making him say what he never said would make the Bible say there is no God when it merely recites the fact the fool hath said this in his heart. Mr. Mann admits the justice of the charge of redundancy of metaphor and illustration, and says it is the fault of his mind, and that if they could only know how much he strives against it they would pity rather than censure.

While all of the masters were not in full sympathy with the tone and temper of the "Remarks" in every particular, the fraternal sentiment led to the signing of them, and all but W. J. Adams stood together loyally. Mr. Mann had an experience at Brown University from which he should have learned to sympathize with the "thirty-one." He was chosen orator of a mock service in the chapel and the college authorities forbade the exercise. Mann did not favor the carrying out of the plans, but when he found that the others would insist he said, "I would better rebel against the college government than against the majority of my fellow students," and so he went ahead with them and delivered his oration. It was this spirit that made the thirty-one Boston masters a unit in their "Remarks."

Mr. Mann's "Reply" was a great surprise to both sides, revealing him in a new light. Such vindictiveness was not supposed to be in his nature. All the intensity of twenty years of political and official life and religious controversy had not called forth upon the combined enemies of all truth, righteousness and progress a hundredth part of the terrors of this "Reply." Its assumptions and assurances were so extravagant, its denunciations so violent, its claims to personal superiority so heroic that it fairly dazed the public and for the moment paralyzed the masters. The masters were in a most uncomfortable and unfortunate position. He had made them appear to antagonize Dr. Samuel G. Howe, Cyrus Pierce, George B. Emerson and others. Like magic the social, intellectual and progressive political leaders rallied as champions of Mr. Mann, who showed himself to be a terrific fighter

and a merciless foe. The peace he offered the
masters, provided they would offer up Barnum
Field as a scapegoat, could not be thought of for
a moment, and Mr. Mann accepted that as a chal-
lenge from the thirty-one. He enlisted the press
very generally against the masters and took a
personal interest in electing members of the
school board who were his ardent friends. It was
decided to have a vigorous examination of the
grammar schools and the masters petitioned the
mayor not to appoint either Dr. Howe or Mr. Brig-
ham for either of the examinations, but he made
each chairman of one of the committees therefor.
Nothing could have been more discomfiting to
the masters or a greater triumph for Mr. Mann,
who advised with the committee regarding the
removal of several of the masters, four of whom
soon retired from the service. When the results
of the examinations, which had no single ray of
cheer in them, were made public eight thousand
copies were printed for free distribution. It was
at such an hour of triumph for Mr. Mann that they
prepared the "Rejoinder" to the "Reply" to the
"Remarks" upon his seventh report.

CHAPTER XII.

"REJOINDER" TO THE "REPLY."

Mr. Barnum Field, respectfully declined to sign the "Rejoinder" because Mr. Mann had said that he was never to be forgiven and they must continue to dwell on opposite sides of the moral universe. In his place appeared a powerful presentation of the case of the thirty-one masters, calm, clear, firm, earnest. The writers of the other sections were Wm. A. Shepard, S. S. Greene, and Joseph Hale.

Read to-day, this first part stands as an unimpeachable indictment of the matter, method and manner of Mr. Mann's "Reply." He is charged with misunderstanding or misrepresenting their "Remarks"; with having accused them of what was farthest from their thought; with having attributed motives of which they never dreamed; with injustice, impatience and ill temper. They lose much, however, from being forced to apologize for what Mr. Mann had made them appear to have said and for having to take the attitude of defence of themselves as well as of their "Remarks." Their great gain was in throwing back upon Mr. Mann every one of the really good points he had made against them. Where he had represented them as falsifiers not worthy to be instructors of youth because they had asserted that he knew nothing of the Boston schools—claiming to have visited these schools twelve times in the five years specified—they show that five of these occasions, by his own admission, were after the writing of the report;

that the other seven had not averaged fifteen minutes each; that one was to examine a map exhibition; one to see the building; one was after school hours; one was after the recitations closed; one at an exhibition; one for the purpose of making a speech; one to hear a lesson in music.

Mr. Mann had made much of the fact that he had frequently visited Mr. Harrington's and Mr. Tower's schools for they were the best in the city, but the former had left teaching before the five years' limit and the latter two years before that.

Mr. Mann's attempt to escape their shaft at his tens of thousands of pupils visited in Prussia on the ground that he had said, "I think I may say" and had not put it positively, is turned upon him with irresistible force because he said, "I think I may say, within bounds, tens of thousands." Mr. Mann is left without one unchallenged personal position and in every way his "Reply" is shown to be more vulnerable than his report. Many of the wonderful methods seen in Prussia, published and glorified as coming from there were in daily use in Boston and had been for four or five years. The masters had been studying these new things from Prussia in advance and had adopted some, and adapted others and his ignorance thereof is made to recoil upon him with much force.

Mr. Shepard's "Rejoinder" is more sarcastic, more brilliant and consequently less effective. He was a young man but talented and specially gifted in controversy and among the many rankling suggestions was the irresistible ridicule in commenting upon the Sunday-school visitation. In attempting to parry the thrust in the "Remarks" where Mr. Shepard had figured out thirty-six days in six weeks, Mr. Mann had insisted that as he had visited Sunday schools these ought to be included and the whole be figured on the basis of forty-two days, which correction Mr. Shepard allows very

graciously but in a decidedly merry vein. Among
the pleasantries of Mr. Shepard is a figuring out
of the "leaps into the air in a Scotch school." In
Mr. Mann's ardent description of this school,
speaking of the enthusiasm, he declares that the
children "actually leap into the air from the energy
of their impulses, and repeat this as often as once
in two minutes on the average," and Mr. Shepard
shows that this must mean three thousand, six
hundred "leaps into the air" or one leap every two
seconds.

Mr. S. S. Greene's "Rejoinder" is a dignified discussion of what has since come to be regarded as
the "word" method of teaching reading, and although "logical," bright and brilliant, it appears
so absurd in the light of modern revelations that
one reads it with impatience. From the first Mr.
Mann had every pedagogical advantage as they
had the personal. He knew that he was in the
right, knew that the new methods in reading,
geography, language and arithmetic were as sure
to come as noon to follow the dawn. There has
scarcely been an idea in all the departures of recent years not embodied in Mr. Mann's seventh
report. Every progressive movement in teaching
words, in using maps, in nature study, in abolish-
ing corporal punishment, in emphasizing the
moral element in education was championed with
intensity by Mr. Mann in his seventh report, fifty
years ago.

Miss Mathilde E. Coffin has made quite a sensation by introducing into the Detroit schools ex-
amples and problems made from the facts daily
presented by the press on the ground that every
example should give some useful information as
well as present opportunity for practice. Mr.
Mann wrote a text-book on arithmetic based on
that idea, pure and simple, nearly half a century
since.

The "Remarks" and the "Rejoinder" were mainly devoted to defending what no power could save and the sentiment of the city realized it. The logical skill and masterly style of these two great documents, together with the fact that every one recognized that they had the advantage of him in the controversy but gave greater emphasis to the truth for which he stood. The strength of these two masterpieces of controversy was their weakness and with the appearance of the "Rejoinder" Mr. Mann's place as an educator was for the first time unchallenged, and the city and the state were ready to do his bidding for the advancement of education. The "Rejoinder" caused no ripple of excitement, the public interest in the controversy had abated, public judgment was made up and language counted for little. Mr. Mann was enthroned as the genius of educational progress and few took the trouble to read what was so well said by his antagonists. It was the old, old story with which the world is so familiar. "There is a tide in the affairs of men, which taken at the flood leads on to fortune."

CHAPTER XIII.

Mr. Mann's "Answer" to the "Rejoinder" shows him in quite a different light. "Richard is himself again." He was certainly not himself when he wrote his "Reply." He admitted afterward that he was driven to the wall and must turn upon his pursuer and vindicate himself. It was an act of desperation. It grieved his friends, who lost no time in rallying to his assistance.

The details of the conflict were taken out of his hands at once. It was seen that he was no better qualified to conduct his own case than a lawyer to plead his own cause or a physician to administer to himself in a high fever. Thirty of the most eminent men of Boston organized themselves at once to withstand the attack of the thirty masters—Mr. Adam's withdrawal having reduced their number to thirty. They took in hand the election of school boards, the naming of committees for the examination of the grammar schools, the removal of inefficient grammar masters,—four of whom were dismissed within two years,—the management of the Legislature and all other matters of this kind. The names of these men were never made public and their cooperation was not known for a long time. The masters thought their triumph was to be sure and speedy. They had every reason so to think, and some of them had said, in the hour of over-confidence, "the board of education is already abolished, we only await the action of the Legislature to record the fact." They soon found, however,

that they were not in a conflict with Mr. Mann but
with the spirit of progress itself, with principali-
ties and powers, with unseen forces, social and
political.

No men or body of men could have won
in such a contest. In it all of Mr. Mann's
grandeur was apparent. His friendships were in
evidence, Josiah Quincy, Charles Sumner, Edward Everett, John G. Whittier, Henry Wilson,
Anson P. Burlingame, Theodore Parker, with
merchants, bankers and professional men, ar-
rayed themselves with him. These thirty at once
raised among themselves $5,000 and asked the
Legislature for a like sum, that thus $10,000 might
be placed in the hands of the Board of Education
for the improvement of the normal schools.
Charles Sumner gave his bond for the payment
of this sum. This was done as a vote of confidence in the board and its secretary and it passed
almost unanimously. For the first time there
was no opposition in the Legislature to the Board
or to anything that it proposed. Indifference to
education everywhere disappeared and even the
state teachers' association that had arranged a
program attacking the Board, read the signs of
the times in season to change the plans and have
no reference to the Board whatever.

Mr. Mann's "Answer" recognized the fact that
he had nothing to fear and although he can
scarcely be accused of being merciful, he was
temperate, and the chastisements which he administered were with the hand of a master. The
"Rejoinder" had explained very fully that the
"Remarks" did not mean what the "Reply" had
made them seem to mean, and he skilfully humil-
iated the masters by accepting their adequate
apology. With the same force he declines to
notice the "bitterness" in the "Rejoinder" on the
ground that bitterness is bitter enough when it is

fresh, but it is intolerable when it is sour. The
"Answer" had little interest then and less now for
it was understood then and is better understood
now that the controversy had been fought out on
general influences rather than in the technicalities of discussion. No one cared how many times
he had visited the Boston schools, for what he
had gone, or with whom. None cared how many
·schools he had visited in six weeks in Prussia nor
how many "leaps into the air" the children made
per minute in the Scotch school; none cared for
the question of veracity or the extent of the flights
of rhetoric or imagination. It was enough that
Mr. Mann had established the principle that
teachers should be trained, that was common
sense; that there should be less corporal punishment, that was common sense also,—the number
of punishments in Boston were reduced eighty
per cent in two years after the "Remarks"; that
he believed in methods in reading, geography and
arithmetic, that looked sensible on the surface,
and the general verdict was that it was vicious for
the masters to annoy him and call him off from
his greater work.

The weakness of his "Reply" and the strength
of the "Remarks" and of the "Rejoinder" concerned no one. The world had its own interests
and concerned itself not the least with the justice
or the injustice of the case, with argumentative
winnings and losings of the disputants. The public formed its judgments by the logic of events
and that verdict glorified Horace Mann and made
him educationally immortal.

There is no better opportunity to study the
hidden forces in society than is presented by the
conditions in Boston in 1843–6 and the experiences of Horace Mann and the thirty-one Boston
masters.

Mr. Mann made an educational crisis. To make

a crisis one must focus public attention upon
some issue; force the opponents to make so clear
a presentation as to satisfy all parties interested;
and convince the disinterested public that the
opposition occupies wholly untenable ground.
This is the highest achievement of a reformer.
No man is great who cannot in the emergency
focus public attention upon his issue, who does
not succeed in getting a mighty presentation of
the opposition, who does not win the disinterested
public. Pitt's fame was largely due to Walpole;
and Disraeli's to Gladstone. Webster's niche is
largely due to the masterly speech of Hayne to
whom he could and did reply, and Lincoln would
never have had the opportunity to immortalize
himself but for the mighty speeches of Stephen
A. Douglas which he answered. Horace Mann
would never have had his place as an educator
but for the controversy with the Boston masters.
Were it possible, as it is not, to rob those two
great documents—the "Remarks" and the "Rejoinder"—of their strength, Mr. Mann would be
robbed largely of his preëminence. His first
five reports and his crusades up and down the
state had focused public attention, but in all those
years there were well-defined suspicions that
his was not a disinterested service, that his wisdom was not without alloy. The Unitarians had
captured most of the churches in and about Boston, they had taken to themselves Harvard college and there were not wanting those who
hinted broadly that Mr. Mann had sectarian
designs on the public schools.

So long as he lectured abstractly, and talked of
reforms that were needed people were willing
that he should talk; when the "Remarks" appeared everybody said, as they did of Walpole a
hundred years earlier, of Gladstone, of Hayne and
of Douglas in their time, "that is unanswerable."

The associates of the masters, like the associates of Walpole and Douglas, rallied about their champions but the disinterested public went with Mr. Mann as it had gone with Mr. Lincoln in the Douglas debates. He had made a crisis and his seventh report was an immortal document; opposition to the normal schools was never more to be heard in the land and oral instruction, the word method and less corporal punishment were certain to come to the Boston schools. He who magnifies those great opposing documents helps to give the crisis maker his place upon the throne.

CHAPTER XIV.

THE STATESMAN.

When Mr. Mann left law and politics for an educational career he lost caste politically. His influence waned. He was not sought for campaigning and the Legislature where he had served for many years heeded his pleadings little more than those of the stranger. Before the echoes of the controversy had died away, Mr. Mann was selected from Daniel Webster's Congressional district to take the seat in Congress made vacant by the sudden death in the House of ex-President John Quincy Adams and that from a district in which he had resided but a short time. It was an honor such as has rarely come to an educator.

From the first he attracted attention in Washington because of his reputation and forensic power. He had been in Congress but a little time when Mr. Webster delivered his famous—many thought infamous—seventh of March speech in which he outraged the political sentiment of Massachusetts. What Mr. Webster thought sure to add to his political prospects and to the business advantage of Boston was interpreted to his disadvantage. Mr. Mann seized the occasion for heroic action. He reasoned, as he afterward admitted, that, with the feeling against Mr. Webster because of this speech, he would not venture to be a candidate for reëlection; if he did, defeat was certain. In view of these conditions Mr. Mann made a vigorous, keen, severe attack upon Mr. Webster which angered that statesman as nothing in his experience had done

before. This was due partly to the fact that it
came when he was unprepared to meet it and
partly because of the audacity of the man, and as
he thought, impropriety of the junior congress-
man administering a rebuke to the senior senator.
The best laid plans sometimes come to naught.
At this juncture President Taylor died, Mr.
Filmore succeeded him, Mr. Webster was made
secretary. of state and became to all intents
and purposes the administration with all the
patronage for New England at his disposal.
Nothing could have been worse for Mr. Mann.
The condemnation was now directed to him and
criticisms, public and private, were showered
upon him. When his term expired and he was up for
reëlection Mr. Webster and the entire party machinery worked against him with such vigor that
he lost the renomination by a single vote. He declared himself an independent candidate, spoke in
every village and hamlet in the district, and was
elected over the regular nominee by a large vote.
This was a personal triumph for Mr. Mann, but
for Mr. Webster it was a personal rebuke which
he felt keenly.

Mr. Mann's congressional record was eminently
creditable and demonstrated his statesmanlike
qualities. At the close of the regulation term in
Congress he was made the candidate of the new
party of Sumner, Wilson, Burlingame and others
for governor. There was no possibility that year
of his election and he put no heart into the cam-
paign. His nomination was made by Henry Wilson and seconded by Anson P. Burlingame in
speeches that were among the noblest tributes
ever offered a candidate. With this he retired
from the political arena where he had won laurels
and had been of great service to humanity. The
brilliancy of this experience added a halo to his
educational service which gave it character and
statesmanlike dignity.

CHAPTER XV.

An inscrutable Providence or a cruel fate led Mr. Mann at the age of fifty-six to accept the presidency of Antioch college, Yellow Springs, Ohio, and attempt the impossible under conditions that chafed and rasped him for the remaining years of his eventful life.

In America there are two sad pictures, an educator out of place at fifty-six and a politician out of a job at any time. Mr. Mann's defeat for the governorship, although in no sense a surprise, left him with no immediate political future, and he may be pardoned if he did not see any educational attractions in New England. Had he rested for a few months many choices would have been presented. The lecture platform, the literary arena or any one of many educational positions would have been available, but the friends of Antioch college had enlisted his sympathies, appealed to his self-sacrificing devotion, magnified the possibilities, misrepresented—let it be hoped unintentionally—the reality, and he took his family out of Massachusetts that he had blessed into an institution, community and conditions which were at that time as ill adapted to him as the depths of the sea to a canary.

Religiously, educationally, politically, socially, philanthropically he was misplaced. His friends have sometimes heaped abuse upon the men and the community that wore him out completely in six years, wrecking him physically and shading every hour of those last years, but it is probable that he was as great a burden to them as they were to him. It is useless to censure, but much charity is required for a worshipper at the shrine of Horace Mann to see his family literally "dumped" homeless and friendless upon the debris of that college yard with no house in the town, no rooms in the building ready for, or approaching readiness, for wife and children, and that was really as bright a day as he saw until his beautiful translation to the Land Immortal from the bosom of his family, August 2, 1858.

He was misplaced but he could not, would not retreat and against the advice of all friends he stayed and hoped against hope, sacrificed religious ideals, personal comforts, home privileges and continued to bury the money of his friends. He fought opposition in an arena where he was at every disadvantage until at the age of sixty-two his spirit seemed to float away in a delightful vision and a glorious inheritance remained for the widow and orphan of one of the most beautiful, grand and noble characters that has blessed this land.

A fractional part of the energy, wisdom, devotion that were wasted at Antioch would have immortalized him as a college president at Williams or at Oberlin, but the history of education has gained much from the failure of his party to win in the gubernatorial contest of 1852 and from the failure to establish an educational institution of national fame in southeastern Ohio for from the public mind the last ten years of his life have faded from memory and all that remains to be more and more glorified are the ten years of sacrifice and devotion, of heroism and wisdom, of talent and genius with which the schools of Massachusetts were blessed, as have been the schools of no other commonwealth. In front of the State House, in storm and sunshine, as a work of art, stands a noble statue of a grand man, but a fitter memorial is the manhood and woman-hood of Massachusetts, all the brighter and better because of the life, the labor and the love of

HORACE MANN.

CHAPTER XVI.

The first question to arise with every reader of these pages thus far will be,—"Why not include the controversy?" The answer is very simple. Because the six principal documents would of themselves require a book twelve times the size of this. All that can be attempted is to give in the concluding chapter a few selections regarding one phase of the contest. The a-b-c will afford as good an illustration as any. This is Mr. Mann's description of the word method or as he styled it, the Prussian way of teaching children to read.

"The teacher first drew a house upon the blackboard. By the side of the drawing and under it, he wrote the word *house.* With a long pointing rod he ran over the form of the letters,—the children, with their slates before them and their pencils in their hands, looking at the pointing rod and tracing the forms of the letters in the air. The next process was to copy the word 'house,' both in script and in print, on their slates. Then followed the formation of the sounds of the letters of which the word was composed, and the spelling of the word. Here the *names* of the letters were not given but only the sounds which those letters have in combination. The letter *h* was first selected and set up in the reading-frame, and the children, instead of articulating our alphabetic *h,* (aitch,) merely gave a hard breathing,—such a sound as the letter really has in the word 'house.' Then the diphthong, *au* (the German word for 'house' is spelled 'haus') was taken and sounded by itself, in the same way. Then the blocks containing *h,* and *au,* were brought together, and the two sounds were combined. Lastly, the letter *s* was first sounded by itself, then added to the others, and then the whole word was spoken. Sometimes the last letter in a word was first taken and sounded,—after that the penultimate,—and so on until the word was completed. The responses of the children were sometimes individual, and sometimes simultaneous, according to a signal given by the master.

"In every such school, also, there are printed sheets or cards, containing the letters, diphthongs and whole words. The children are taught to sound a diphthong, and then asked in what words that sound occurs. On some of these cards there are words enough to make several short sentences, and when the pupils are a little advanced, the teacher points to several isolated words in succession, which when taken together make a familiar sentence, and thus he gives them an agreeable surprise, and a pleasant initiation into reading.

"After the word 'house' was thus completely impressed upon the minds of the children, the teacher drew his pointing rod over the lines which formed the house; and the children imitated him, first in the air, while they were looking at his motions, then on their slates. In their drawings there was of course a great variety as to taste and accuracy; but each seemed pleased with his own, for their first attempts had never been so criticised as to produce discouragement. Several children were then called to the blackboard to draw a house with chalk. After this, the teacher entered into a conversation about houses."

"Compare the above method with that of calling up a class of abecedarians,—or, what is more common, a single child, and, while the teacher holds a book or a card before him, and, with a

pointer in his hand, says, *a,* he echoes *a;* then *b,*
and he echoes *b;* and so on until the vertical row of
lifeless and ill-favored characters is completed,
and then of remanding him to his seat, to sit still
and look at vacancy. If the child is bright, the
time which passes during this lesson is the only
part of the day when he does not think. Not a
single faculty of the mind is occupied except that
of imitating sounds; and even the number of these
imitations amounts only to twenty-six. A parrot
or an idiot could do the same thing. And so of
the organs and members of the body. They are
condemned to inactivity;—for the child who
stands most like a post is most approved; nay, he
is rebuked if he does not stand like a post. A
head that does not turn to the right or left, an eye
that lies moveless in its socket, hands hanging
motionless at the side, and feet immovable as
those of a statue, are the points of excellence,
while the child is echoing the senseless table of a,
b, c. As a general rule, six months are spent before the twenty-six letters are mastered, though
the same child would learn the names of twenty-
six playmates or twenty-six playthings in one or
two days."

"The practice of beginning with the 'Names of
Letters,' is founded upon the idea that it facili-
tates the combination of them into words. On
the other hand, I believe that if two children, of
equal quickness and capacity, are taken, one of
whom can name every letter of the alphabet, at
sight, and the other does not know them from
Chinese characters, the latter can be most easily
taught to read,—in other words, that learning the
letters first is an absolute hindrance."

"The letter *a,* says Worcester, has seven sounds,
as in *fate, fat, fare, far, fast, fall, liar.* In the
alphabet, and as a name, it has but one,—the long
sound. Now suppose the words of our language

in which this letter occurs, to be equally divided among these seven classes. The consequence must be that as soon as the child begins to read, he will find one word in which the letter *a* has the sound he has been taught to give it, and six words in which it has a different sound. If, then, he follows the instruction he has received, he goes wrong six times to going right once. Indeed, in running over a score of his most familiar words,— such as *papa, mama, father, apple, hat, cat, rat, ball, fall, call, warm, swarm, man, can, pan, ran, brass, glass, water, star,* etc., he does not find, in a single instance, that sound of *a* which he has been taught to give it in the alphabet."

"Did the vowels adhere to their own sounds, the difficulty would be greatly diminished. But, not only do the same vowels appear in different dresses, like masqueraders, but, like harlequins, they exchange garbs with each other. How often does *e* take the sound of *a*, as in *there, where,* etc.; and *i*, the sound of *e;* and *o*, the sound of *u;* and *u*, the sound of *o;* and *y*, the sound of *i.*

"In one important particular the consonants are more perplexing than the vowels. The very definition of a consonant, as given in the spelling-books, is, 'a letter which has no sound, or only an imperfect one, without the help of a vowel.' And yet the definers themselves, and the teachers who follow them, proceed immediately to give a perfect sound to all the consonants."

"I believe it is within bounds to say, that we do not sound the letters in reading once in a hundred times as we were taught to sound them when learning the alphabet. Indeed, were we to do so in one tenth part of the instances, we should be understood by nobody. What analogy can be pointed out between the rough breathing of the letter *h*, in the words *when, where, how,* etc., and the "name-sound" (aytch, aitch, or aych, as it is given by different spelling-book compilers) of that letter, as it is taught from the alphabet?

"This subject might be further illustrated by reference to other languages,—the Greek, for instance. Will the names of the letters, *kappa, omicron, sigma, mu, omicron, sigma,* make the word *kosmos?* And yet these letters come as near making that word, as those given by the Rev. Mr. Ottiwell Wood, at a late trial in Lancashire, England, did to the sound of his own name. On Mr. Wood's giving his name to the court, the judge said, 'Pray, Mr. Wood, how do you spell your name?' to which the witness replied;—'O double T, I double U, E double L, double U, double O, D.' In the anecdote it is added, that the learned judge at first laid down his pen in astonishment; and then, after making two or three unsuccessful attempts, declared he was unable to record it."

To this the Masters made extended reply in their "Remarks" from which the following statement is selected:—

"When we speak of words, we may mean either the *audible,* or the *written* signs of our ideas. The term *word* is, therefore, ambiguous, unless it be so qualified as to have a specific reference. In speaking of familiar words, nothing can be meant except that the child can *utter* them; he knows them only as *audible* signs. To say that *printed* words are familiar to a child's tongue, can have no other meaning than that he is accustomed to the taste of ink; to say that such words are familiar to his *ear,* is to attribute to that ink, a tongue; and to say that they are familiar to the mind, is to suppose the child already able to read. Now, as reading aloud is nothing less than translating *written* into *audible* signs, a knowledge of the latter, whatever may be the system of teaching, is presupposed to exist, and is about as necessary to the one learning to read, as would be a knowledge of the English language to one who would translate Greek into English.

"To illustrate. Take the printed word *mother;* when pronounced, it is familiar 'to the ear, the tongue, and the mind.' Does this familiarity aid the child in the least, in comprehending the printed picture? Can he, from his acquaintance with the audible sign, utter that sign by looking upon the six unknown letters which spell it?

"The truth is, in all that belongs, appropriately, to the question under consideration, the word is unknown; unknown as a whole, unknown in all its parts, and unknown as to the mode of combining those parts. The question, when restricted to its appropriate limits, is simply this; 'What is the best method of teaching a child to comprehend *printed* words?'"

"Is the rose any the less agreeable to the mind of the child, or, is the word *rose,* when pronounced, any the less familiar to his organs of speech or to his ear, because its printed sign is learned by combining the letters r-o-s-e? Or does the mere act of telling the child to say *rose,* while pointing to the picture, formed of four unknown letters, in any way enhance its agreeableness?

"The question, then, is not whether a child shall be 'introduced to a stranger through the medium of old acquaintances,' for, in fact, by the new system, this introduction is made through the medium of the teacher's voice.

"The true question at issue is, whether the child shall be furnished with an attendant to announce the name of the stranger, or whether he shall be furnished with *letters* of introduction by which, unattended, he may make the acquaintance, not of some seven hundred strangers merely, but of the whole seventy thousand unknown members of our populous vocabulary."

"When the secretary, in speaking of a child after the first year of his life, says that, then, 'the wonderful faculty of language begins to develop itself,' he undoubtedly refers to spoken language. And well may that be called a wonderful faculty by which, through the agency of the vocal organs, we can so modify *mere sounds,* as to send them forth freighted with thoughts which may cause the hearts of others to thrill with ecstatic delight, or throb with unutterable anguish. And no wonder that there should have existed, early in the history of the world, a desire to enchain and represent to the eye these evanescent messengers of thought. Hence the early and rude attempts at writing, by means of pictures and symbols. But these, unfortunately, were representatives of the *message,* not the *messenger;* of the idea, not the sound which conveys it. At length arose that wonderful *invention,* the art of representing to the eye, by means of letters, the component parts of a *spoken word,* so that now, not merely the *errand,* but the *bearer* stands pictured before us. The grand and distinctive feature of this invention is, that it establishes a connection between the *written* and the *audible* signs of our ideas. It throws, as it were, a bridge across the otherwise impassable gulf which must ever have separated the one from the other. The hieroglyphics and symbols of the ancients performed but one function. To those who, by a purely arbitrary association, were able to pass from the sign to the thing signified, they were representatives of ideas—and ideas *merely;* hence they are called ideographic characters, and that mode of writing has been denominated the *symbolic,* and is exemplified in the Chinese language."

"The new system of teaching reading abandons entirely the distinctive feature of the phonetic mode of writing, and our words are treated as though they were capable of performing but one function, that of representing ideas. The language, although written with alphabetic characters, becomes, to all intents and purposes, a symbolic language. Now we say, as ours is designedly a phonetic language, no system of teaching ought to meet with public favor, that strips it of its principal power. And we confess ourselves not a little surprised that the secretary, who cherishes such correct views of the inferiority of the Chinese language, should urge us to convert ours into Chinese."

"As our language was written with alphabetic characters, our words are too long and cumbrous for becoming mere symbols. A single character would be vastly superior to our *trisyllables* and *polysyllables*. If the new system prevails, we may soon expect a demand for reform in this respect. As it now is, the child must meet with all the difficulties that necessarily accompany the acquisition of the Chinese language, and these greatly increased by the forms of our words.

"The defenders of the new system seem to lose sight of the nature and design of the alphabetic mode of writing, as an *invention.* To understand an invention, we must first know the law of nature which gave rise to it, and then the several parts of the invented system, as well as the adaptation of these parts, when combined, to accomplish some useful purpose. Thus, to explain the steam-engine, the chemical law by which water is converted into steam must first be understood, and in connection with it, that of elasticity, common to all aëriform bodies. Then follows—what constitutes the main point in this illustration—the explanation of the several parts of the machine, with the modes of combining them, so as to gain that immense power, which is found so valuable in the arts. Take another illustration, more nearly allied to the subject under consideration. It was discovered a few years since, that a piece of iron exposed, under given circumstances, to a galvanic current, would become a powerful magnet, and that it would cease to be such, the instant the current was intercepted. Little was it then thought, that this simple discovery would give rise to an invention by which the winged lightning, fit messenger of thought, could be employed to enable the inhabitants of Maine to converse with their otherwise distant neighbors in Louisiana, with almost as much ease, as though the parties were seated in the same parlor.

"Now, no one will pretend, that to make use of the steam-engine successfully, all that is necessary is to gain an idea of it, as a *whole.* The several parts, with their various relations and combinations, must be explained. Equally necessary is it, in managing the magnetic telegraph, for the operator to be familiar with the laws of electricity, and the adaptation of the several parts of the machine, to accomplish, by means of that agent, the object proposed. But who would think of interpreting the results of its operation, the dots, the lines, the spaces, by looking upon them as constituting a single picture?

"To apply these illustrations. It was discovered, ages ago, that Nature had endowed the organs of speech with the power of uttering a limited number of simple sounds. From this discovery originated the invention of letters to represent these elementary sounds. Letters constitute the *machinery* of the invention. They are the *tools* by which the art of reading is to be acquired; and a thorough knowledge of letters bears the same relation to reading, as does the thorough acquaintance with the parts of a steam-engine, or of the magnetic telegraph to a skilful use of these instruments. The new system proposes to abandon, for a time at least, all that is peculiar to this invention; all that distinguishes it from the rude and unphilosophical systems of symbolic writing, which, centuries ago, gave place to it, throughout every portion of the civilized world. Now, since such an estimate was placed upon this invention by the ancients, as to secure its adoption to the exclusion of all other methods of writing; and since a trial of many centuries has served only to confirm mankind in the belief of its superiority over every other system; we can but protest against the adoption of a mode of teaching, that subjects the child to such inconvenience and loss."

"The word *letter,* as applied to the alphabet, is ambiguous, unless accompanied by some term, or explanatory phrase, to show what is intended. In referring to one of the elementary sounds which enters into the formation of a *spoken* word, we call that *sound* a letter; so, in speaking of the conventional sign, which represents that sound to the eye, as the character *h,* seen in a *printed* word, that sign we call a letter; both the sound and the sign, take the *name aitch,* for example; this *name,* in turn, is called a letter. Now, to prevent confusion, these three things, the power, the character, and the name, should be kept entirely distinct from each other. In a *spoken* word, elementary *sounds* are combined; in a *written* word, elementary *characters;* in neither written nor spoken words, are the *names* of letters joined, except in those instances, where the name and power are the same, as in the case of the long sounds of the vowels."

"We never supposed, nor do we know of a single advocate of the old system, who ever supposed, that the *names* of letters entered into the formation of words; as, h-a-t, into *aitchaitee;* 'l-e-g,' into 'elegy.'

"Names were not given to letters for such a purpose. They were assigned to them, for the same reason that names are given to other objects, to aid us in referring to the objects themselves. One would scarcely expect to convince even a child, that there was neither pastry, fruit, cinnamon, nor sugar, in the pie he was eating, by telling him that pies are never made of such names as *pastry, cinnamon,* etc."

"To neglect the names of letters is to destroy, at once, one of the most important exercises of the primary school; that is, oral spelling.   That letters must have names to aid us in referring to them, no one will deny."

"If letters must have names, why should the child be kept in ignorance of them?   One of the first inquiries of a child, on seeing a new object is, 'What is it?'   'What do you call it?' or, in other words, 'What is its name?'   Shall such inquiries be silenced, when made respecting the alphabet?"

"Mr. Mann says: 'If *b,* is *bc,* then *bc* is *bee,* the name of an insect; and if *l* is *cl,* then *cl* is *eel,* the name of a fish;' that is to say, if the object named, is the same as the name itself, then that name becomes the name of an insect, or of a fish.   Surprising!

"All printed names of objects are formed from printer's ink. *Bee* is the printed name of an object; and since the object itself is the same as its name, it follows that this insect is only printer's ink. It is, therefore, harmless, unless it is that remarkable bee that has three stings; for we are told that—

" '*No bee* has two stings;' and that, 'one bee has one more sting than no bee (and perhaps, this one) has three stings.

"As for the *eel,* fit emblem of the logic that caught it, we will leave it to hands best able to retain it."

"Since the child cannot 'appreciate the remote

benefits' of learning the alphabet, must his caprice govern those who can, and determine them to abandon, even for a time, what they know is all-important in teaching him to read? A child is sick, and cannot appreciate the remote, or immediate benefits of taking disagreeable medicine. Will a judicious parent, who is fully sensible of the child's danger, regard, for one moment, his wishes, to save him from a little temporary disquietude? A child has no fondness for the dry and uninteresting tables of arithmetic. Shall he, therefore, be gratified in his desire to hasten on to the solution of questions, before acquiring such indispensable pre-requisites? We have been accustomed to suppose that the responsibilities of the teacher's profession, consist, mainly, in his being required to fashion the manners and tastes of his pupils, to promote habits of thinking and patient toil, and to give direction to their desires and aspirations, rather than to minister to the gratification of their passion for pleasure."

"To *gratify* the child, should not be the teacher's aim, but rather to lay a permanent foundation, on which to rear a noble and well-proportioned super-structure. If, while doing *this,* the teacher is successful in rendering mental *exertion* agreeable, and in leading the child from one conquest to another, till *achievement itself* affords delight, it is well; such pleasure stimulates to greater exertion. But if, to cultivate pleasure-seeking is his aim, he had better, at once, abandon his profession, and obtain an employment in which he will not endanger the welfare, both of individuals and society, by sending forth a sickly race, palsied in every limb, through idleness, a vain attempt to gratify a morbid thirst for pleasure.

"The new system proposes to afford the child pleasure in the exercise of *reading words;* yet, instead of requiring him to exert, in the least, his mental faculties, in combining the elementary parts of these words, the teacher gives merely the result of his own mental processes, and exacts nothing from the child, but a passive reception of the sound, which is to be associated arbitrarily, with the *visible picture,* pointed out to him."

"To this method of teaching we are opposed, for the following reasons:

1st.—"Teaching whole words according to this plan, to any extent whatever, gives the child no facility for learning new ones. Every word must be taken upon authority, until the alphabet is learned.

2d.—"Since the alphabet must, at some period, be acquired, with all its imperfections, it is but a poor relief, to compel the child, at first, to associate seven hundred different, arbitrary forms with the ideas which they represent, and then to learn the alphabet itself."

3d.—"Another objection to converting our language into Chinese, arises from the *change* which must inevitably take place in the modes of associating the printed word with the idea which it represents, when the child is taught to regard words as composed of elements. Children, at first, learn to recognize the word, by the new method, as a single picture, not as composed of parts; and for aught we know, they begin in the middle of it and examine each way. It is not probable that they proceed invariably from left to right, as in the old mode. However that may be, an entire change must take place when they begin to learn words, as composed of letters. The attention, then, is directed to the parts of which words are composed. While the eye is employed in combining the visible characters, the mind unites the powers which they represent, and the organs of speech are prompt to execute what the eye and the mind have simultaneously prepared for them. The mode of association in a symbolic language, if we mistake not, is this: The single picture is associated arbitrarily, yet directly, with the *idea;* the *idea* is then associated with its audible sign; this sign, being familiar to the child, is readily uttered. In a phonetic language, it is different. The attention being directed to the letters and their powers, the child is conducted immediately to the audible sign; this when uttered, or thought of, suggests the idea. Whether or not these are the correct views, is immaterial to the argument. All that is claimed is, that a *change* takes place in the modes of association, as soon as the child begins to combine letters into words. It is of this *change* we complain. All will acknowledge the importance of forming in the child, correct habits of association, such as will not need revolutionizing at a subsequent period in life."

4th.—"The new system fails to accomplish the object which it proposes. The main design of this mode of teaching seems to be, to escape the ambiguity arising from the variety of sounds which attach to some of the letters, as well as from the variety of forms by which the same sounds may be represented.

"The defenders of this system seem to forget, since these anomalies are elementary, that they must be carried into the formation of words. Thus, we can represent a single elementary sound, first by *a,* then by *ai,* and again, by *ei;* hence, we can form three different words; as *vane, vain, vein.* In a similar manner we have, *rain, reign, rein; wright, write, right, rite;* and hundreds of others. It will be seen at once, that it must be as difficult for a child to attach the same sound to four different pictures called words, as to four different pictures called letters. Hence, it is plain, that *we have 'harlequins' among words; as well as among letters.* The only difference is, that the former are more numerous, yet the legitimate offspring of the latter. We have 'masqueraders,' too, among words. Let the sound represented by the four letters, r-i-t-e, fall upon the child's ear, and he may think, either, of a ceremony, of making letters with a pen, of justice, or of a workman. Again, let either the printed or spoken word *pound,* for example, be given; and he may think of an enclosure for stray cattle, of striking a blow, of certain weights, as avoirdupois, apothecaries', or Troy weight, and also, of a denomination of money."

5th.—"It introduces confusion into the different grades of schools.

"The elements must be taught somewhere. If neglected in the primary schools, they must be taught in the grammar schools. And thus the order of things is reversed, and disarrangement introduced into the whole school system. The teacher who is employed, and paid, for instructing in the higher branches, is compelled to devote time and attention to the studies appropriately belonging to the schools of a lower grade."

"Two children, in like circumstances, in every respect, commence learning to read; the first learns some seven hundred different words, as he would so many different letters; having acquired no more ability to learn the seven hundred and first, than he had at the beginning; afterwards he learns the twenty-six letters of the alphabet, including all the 'harlequins' and 'masqueraders,' and finally the art of combining the letters into words. The other learns first, the letters; then, the art of combining them; and finally makes use of this knowledge, to acquire his seven hundred words. Now by what rule of arithmetic, or of common sense, it is ascertained that the former will advance more rapidly than the latter, is to us entirely unknown."

"The main question at issue, we are constrained to answer in the negative. The arguments abduced in its support are, as we believe, inconclusive. The plausibility of some arises from considerations wholly irrelevant; others are fallacious; and others still, are based upon false premises.

"On the contrary, the reasons brought against the change, and in favor of the prevailing system, are of paramount importance. Therefore, as conscientious and faithful servants in the cause of education, we feel bound to adhere to the path of duty, rather than yield to the opinions even of those who are high in authority."

The "Reply" of Mr. Mann deals with the question in this way:—

"There are several reasons why I shall not attempt a lengthened reply to this part of the 'Remarks.' The first is, that, from beginning to end, it is an arrant misrepresentation of the system it professes to impugn. I have never advocated, or known, or heard of, nor have I met any person who has ever advocated, or known, or heard of, any such mode of teaching the English language to children, as the 'Remarks' assail."

"It would be useless to consider, in detail, those arguments which are brought to overthrow a system which nobody upholds. Besides, the plain, common-sense views which belong to this subject, are turned into metaphysics, by the 'Remarks,' and treated with division and subdivision, that bewilder instead of elucidating. The subject is ground down, and pulverized into impalpability, —beyond microscopic vision. Had it been the unaided production of a single mind, the subtlety and evanescence of its refinements might have been less;—now, I know not how otherwise to describe it than as the doctrine of metaphysics applied to the almost endless anomalies of the alphabet. An attempt to individualize the atomical parts of this section, and to give an answer to each, would be like attempting to beat back a league-square of sea-fog, by hitting each particle with the sharpened end of a rod. I shall content myself, therefore, with endeavoring to find some *nuclei* rarified into less metaphysical tenuity than the general mass, and striking at them."

"By the 'old method,' the names of the letters,—the A, B, C, as they have been immemorially called,—were first taught. After these letters, came tables of ab and eb, of bla and ble, of ska, ske, of bam, flam, etc., etc., an almost endless catalogue, and doleful as endless."

"By the 'old system,' when the child could master the alphabet at sight, and could read these names of nothing, by spelling them, he was put to the reading of short sentences. Then, and not till then, was any order or beauty evolved to his vision, out of night and chaos. From inquiries made, I know not of how many teachers, I learn that it has taken children, on an average, at least six months to master the alphabet, on this plan, even when they went to school constantly. In country districts, where there are short schools and long vacations, it has generally required a year, and often eighteen months, to teach a child the twenty-six letters of the alphabet; when the same child would have learned the names of twenty-six playmates, or of twenty-six interesting objects of any kind, in one or two days. And the reason is obvious. In learning the meaningless letters of the alphabet, there was nothing to attract his attention, to excite his curiosity, to delight his mind, or to reward his efforts. The life, the zest, the eagerness with which all children, except natural-born idiots, seek for real objects, ask their names, or catch them without asking, never enlivened this process. The times of the lessons were seasons of suspended animation. The child was taught *not to think.* His eyes and mind were directed to objects as little interesting as so many grains of sand. For the time being, he was banished from this world into the realms of vacuity. By the letters and abs, no glimmer of an idea was excited in the child's mind, and when he was put into words and short sentences, he found, as the general rule, that the letters had all changed their names, without any act of the Legislature. Were the common objects of nature or of art,—animals, trees, flowers, fruits, articles of furniture and of dress, implements of trade, etc., etc., learned as slowly as this, an individual would hardly be able to name the objects immediately around him during the first century of his existence; and antediluvian longevity would find him inquiring the names of things now familiar to a child. But all who have arrived at middle life, and been educated in this community, know bitterly what the 'old method' means.

"By the 'new method,' a book is used which contains, short, familiar words, which are the names of pleasant objects or qualities, or suggest the idea of agreeable actions. A simple story is told, or some inquiry is made, in which a particular word is used, and when the child's attention is gained and his interest excited, the word is shown to him, as a whole. He is made to speak it, and is told that the written or printed object means what we mean when we speak the word; and that if he will learn words, he can read such stories in books as he has heard, or speak to people a hundred miles distant from him, or that he can do some other of the hundred wonderful things which belong to reading, and which even a child can be made to understand. Words are shown, which excite pleasant images when spoken, and after a little while, if the instruction is judiciously managed, the child comes to look upon a book as a magic casket, full of varied and beautiful treasures, which he longs to see. Pleasant associations with the book, the school, and the teacher, are created. The idea that every word has a signification is kept perpetually before his mind, until he looks habitually for a meaning in printed words, as much as he does in those spoken ones, which are addressed to him. His mind is kept in an active, thinking state. The time never is, when he looks at the words in a book without going out, in imagination, to things, actions, or relations, beyond the book. He is not stultified as he is when compelled to look at letters and particles, for a year, which are almost nothing in themselves and suggest nothing beyond themselves. After a number of words have been taught in this way,—more or less, according to the capacities of the child, but ordinarily, I should say, less than a hundred,—some of the letters are pointed out. In subsequent lessons the attention is turned more and more to the letters, until all are learned."

There is no occasion to quote from the forty pages devoted to this subject in the "Rejoinder of the Masters," nor from the almost equal space given to it in the "Answer" of Mr. Mann. It now becomes little more than a personal quarrel between the two forces as to which has outraged and misrepresented the other most brutally or skillfully, as you please, and with that we have no concern. The three presentations here made show the relative positions of the contestants. In this phase of the discussion, Mr. Mann is at his best and the masters are at their worst and it is due Mr. Mann, in a study of his life, that the section chosen should be that in which he appears to advantage. It has been said with much plainness

in these pages that he was not creditably represented in the personal issues raised; it is only fair
that the professional side be presented, for in that
he had every advantage.

Time has placed him upon the educational
throne. In the grounds in front of the State
House stand two statues—one of Daniel Webster
and the other of Horace Mann, the only person
in Massachusetts whose antagonism in speech and
politics led to Mr. Webster's thorough discomfiture.
Their differences are forgotten, and admirers of
the statesman-orator and of the statesman-edu-
cator honor them equally. Mr. Mann's statue is
in the most commanding spot in the city of Boston
where his fame is at its height and the Boston
masters of half a century have been rearing immortal monuments to the wisdom and devotion
of the greatest educator of his time. Nowhere
are his praises sung more spiritedly in this
memorial year than by the schools in which children are ennobled and inspired intellectually and
morally by the Boston masters and their corps of
assistants. As the statues of Webster and Mann
stand side by side, placed there by the same authorities, admirers of both, so the Boston schools
of to-day are monuments to Mr. Mann and the
masters who are alike respected for their service.
The men of Massachusetts in this hour of her
commercial, educational and civic grandeur are
the "next generation,"

THE CLIENTS OF HORACE MANN.

Printed in the United States
107383LV00002B/8/A

9 780548 116067